The Wise Body

The Wise Body

Conversations with Experienced Dancers

Edited by Jacky Lansley and Fergus Early

intellect Bristol, UK / Chicago, USA

First published in the UK in 2011 by
Intellect, The Mill, Parnall Road, Fishponds, Bristol, BS16 3JG, UK

First published in the USA in 2011 by
Intellect, The University of Chicago Press, 1427 E. 60th Street,
Chicago, IL 60637, USA

A catalogue record for this book is available from the
British Library.

Cover designer: Holly Rose
Copy-editor: Rebecca Vaughan-Williams
Index: Lyn Greenwood
Typesetting: Mac Style, Beverley, E. Yorkshire

ISBN 978-1-84150-418-6

Printed in the UK by Latimer Trend, Plymouth.

For Ursula

Contents

Acknowledgements

We would like to thank the following institutions and individuals for their help and support with various aspects of assembling and writing this book: firstly of course the interviewees themselves who have been unstintingly generous, not only in giving their time and thought to the interviews and the editing process, but also in pursuing photographs and in certain cases tracing photographers for permissions; then the Daiwa and Sasakawa Foundations and the Winston Churchill Memorial Trust, all of whom supported our research trip to Japan; the Royal Exchange Theatre, Manchester, for housing our interview with Philippe Priasso; all at Green Candle Dance Company and the Dance Research Studio for their generous support. Of the many individuals we have cause to be grateful to, we would like to particularly mention Yoko Nishimura for her role as our interpreter in Japan and for her technical support with all IT matters; Hugo Glendinning for invaluable help with preparing photographs; Professor Ramsay Burt, Ken Bartlett, Rosemary Butcher, Dr Vida Midgelow, Dr Jane Bacon and Nigel Stewart for their helpful advice and encouragement; Senzo and Minosuke Nishikawa for their generous time and hospitality and our good friends Peter Fluck and Anne-Cécile de Bruyne for innumerable dinners during our working stints on the book in Cornwall. Finally we would like to thank all at Intellect Books whose thoroughness and courtesy have helped to make the process of publishing this book an enjoyable experience.

Introduction

Jacky Lansley and Fergus Early

These interviews are the personal voices and words of twelve mature dance practitioners. They convey experience very directly, with a subjective precision that can only come from the artists themselves. There has been much written about dance in the last twenty years, which is helping to place it more clearly within the cultural landscape, yet comparatively little of the writing has been by practising dancers and it could be argued that a discussion of the complex and varied languages of the body in dance, the science of its craft and the knowledge distilled within its lore has been somewhat neglected. This book is inspired by the idea that everyone in the dance community, and many beyond it, will benefit if the voices of experienced practitioners are heard.

We have tried to cast our net wide. Our interviewees include White British, British Asian, White American, African American, Dutch, French, Japanese and Spanish practitioners. The age range, despite the fact that all contributors are 'mature' dancers, is quite extensive – roughly from mid-forties to mid-eighties at the time of interview. The interviews themselves were recorded at different times over several years – the project itself coming to reflect the themes of longevity and continuation that are central to the book.

Two different points became very clear as we began to assemble and compare material: first, the obvious one of diversity, and second, the more surprising one of connectivity. The voices are certainly diverse. Most of our interviews were conducted in English, even when this was not our interviewee's first language, (the exceptions were La Tati and Yoshito Ohno, both of whom we interviewed with interpreters, and Philippe Priasso, whom we interviewed in a mixture of French and English). The different character of language we encountered in these interviews was remarkable; it may not be too fanciful to relate each verbal style to the speaker's mode of dance: Will Gaines, for example, speaks with some of the sharp and fast rhythmic intensity and exuberant improvisation that characterizes his jazz tap. Parts of what Yoshito Ohno said came out, even in translation, as something close to poetry and so we have rendered some passages in short 'poetic' lines, to reflect his verbal style. At all events, the range of language was both a delight and a real challenge to preserve through the long processes of transcription and editing.

And as for connectivity, some connections are not so surprising. We, (your editors) have danced with, taught, been taught by, six of the contributors: Julyen Hamilton, Pauline de Groot, Lisa Nelson, Jane Dudley, Yoshito Ohno and Steve Paxton. The connections here, for us, came through the early days of the London Contemporary Dance School and through the UK New Dance scene as it developed at X6 Dance Space,[2] at the Dartington Dance Festivals[1] and in the pages of our magazine, *New Dance*.[3] But how strange for us one-time ballet dancers to discover that one of Bisakha Sarker's most formative teachers, Uday Shankar, in the Calcutta of her youth, was a dancer who toured with that greatest of twentieth-century balletic icons, Anna Pavlova. Or that Bisakha could connect her English and her Indian experiences through the medium of Lisa Ullman, disciple of Laban – Laban, whose partner and muse had once been Mary Wigman, whose school Jane Dudley attended in her youth in New York. Jane, too, talks of Erick Hawkins as an intrusive male into the hitherto all-female environment of the early Graham company, while Pauline de Groot speaks of him in what seems almost like a different incarnation, as a teacher of a soft, release-based dance style in the early 1960s. Other connections emerge: the profound explorations in improvisation shared by several contributors, the ubiquity of the disciplines of yoga and T'ai Chi and the prevalence of non-dance practices as training, ranging from farming and cleaning to running and swimming.

All the artists interviewed have a solid portfolio of work and a certain recognized status within their varied spheres. All are building on youthful work – as artists quite naturally do within other art forms, recognizing that real development of one's art form takes time; the interviews reveal that, like many dancers, we all struggle with resources, and cope with less financial and other kinds of reward than practitioners with equivalent experience in other fields; however this seems to have given us a strength and an ability to adapt which can sustain. In his interview Will Gaines reminds us that Eartha Kitt had been a dancer '… and so she knows how to go up and down' – which seems to speak for us all. Like everyone, dancers struggle with the almost universal barriers of common prejudice – the isms of race, class, gender and age, to name but a few. Dance has had in the West in the twentieth and early twenty-first century, one great advantage: many of the major figures have been women. Arguably gender has been less of a site for oppressive exclusion than it has in other areas of the arts and society. Class is trickier. Ballet, for example, has historically been performed by artists of working-class origin for owning class audiences. Modern and postmodern dance has been less class-bound. Race is certainly an issue, both in funding and in access to the profession. Up to very recently the majority of ballet companies did not employ any visibly black artists. But of all the oppressions, the one that hits dance hardest is ageism and it is the last to be explicitly addressed.

Western theatre dance has always been obsessed with sexuality – a chronology of costume design for dance could be seen as a kind of strip-tease with its progressive exposure of bodies in more and more revealing clothes moulded tighter and tighter to the bodies' contours. This sexual fantasy world has always demanded that dance be constantly replenished with a supply of fresh young bodies, threatening and ousting more mature artists. As a result, there is within ballet today a ceiling of perhaps 40 for the men and 35 for the women.

By contrast, the modern and postmodern dance of the twentieth and early twenty-first centuries has thrown up some striking examples of the older dancer, or, in most cases the older dancer-choreographer. Most obvious of these are two giants: Merce Cunningham and Martha Graham who danced into their 90s. In another context, the Japanese Butoh dancer, Kazuo Ohno, whose son, Yoshito, is interviewed here, performed into his 100th year. Many of the first generation of postmodern dancers (including some contributors to this book) are now in their 60s or 70s and showing no inclination to retire, or even semi-retire into a teaching role in the traditional way.

However, there is no way that ageism in dance can be discussed without reference to the ageism that pervades society in general. In some respects things are improving: In several countries an enforceable retirement age has been abolished. Demographics have altered drastically, with rapidly rising life expectancy in the developed world tilting the bulk of whole nations' populations towards the older end of the scale. In many countries, people over 50 will soon be a majority of the population. One effect of this shift is that the provision that many governments made for older people's later years – state pensions – can no longer be sustained for the ever-increasing number of years that people are living. As a result, we are certain to need to work longer and retire later. For those of us who define at least a significant part of ourselves as *performer* (and who derive a significant part of our income from performing), it will mean that we are likely to perform for more years because we have to – and perhaps too because we are fitter and in effect 'younger' than previous generations were at the same age.

The contributors to this book, like many of our peers, are engaged in valuable creative research about our bodies, health, art, the environment, and the major ethical and philosophical questions that confront human beings. Some of the work links art and science of the body in a most profound way. Some of the practitioners could legitimately be called philosophers. Some are in fact, while being dancers, making the most interesting 'theatre' today, as physical craft shifts the focus away from an exclusive preoccupation with text. Somehow everyone knows the value of dance – and yet dancers tend not to be valued for their work and research. Those of us who develop a voice and write and talk as well as dance are told we 'think too much' – as though thinking is somehow not part of the practice of dancing. It is a political and social, not just artistic, issue that dancers are supposed to be young, silent, humble and exploitable.

In 1996 Green Candle Dance Company[4] assembled a cast of five dancers, all professionals, all with long and distinguished careers as dancers, creative artists and teachers to collaborate on devising a production in response to this debate. The performers' ages ranged from their 40s to their 80s; Fergus Early, director of the project was himself 50 at the time. As part of the process of developing ideas for the production, entitled *Tales from the Citadel*,[5] Early interviewed each of the collaborators. Small sections of these interviews formed part of the soundtrack for *Tales from the Citadel*, and the process provided inspiration for this book. From the original interviews we retained only that by Jane Dudley. We selected others according to criteria that included: that they should be remarkable performers, still performing, that they are articulate and aware thinkers and that between them they represent a range of styles, cultures and approaches to dance. It also turned out that almost all the artists continuing to perform were also creative artists. It was as if the imperative to make work invoked the energy to perform it. Or perhaps just that these artists had always been their own principal interpreters: the two processes have always been one, in fact.

As we get older we juggle to integrate the various areas of our lives – careers, relationships, homes, finances, caring for others whether children, older relatives or friends. With maturity, complexity adopts us whether or not we choose it. Being an artist in the centre of all this can be extremely difficult; a successful balancing act will often depend on how much personal support one gets. Being a performer as well as a choreographer is of course even more demanding, as we have to 'fit in' physical training, whatever form that training takes. Many dancers' professional lives are so short that they barely get beyond obedience to those disciplines they grew up with, diligently practising their barrework or their floorwork up to the day they walk away from their careers at the majestic age of 35 or 40. But for those who continue, new disciplines, new ways of incorporating the world at large into their dance practice must be found.

Being older, even a bit older in dance seems to nurture more specialized and individualized approaches to training. From the interviews it emerged that there was a great diversity of training practised among the different interviewees. Most of us, as young dancers, had been used to a routine of daily class, taught by a teacher in a specific technique. As time went on, though, and we were no longer part of schools or companies where such disciplines were on offer, our methods of training diverged and became idiosyncratic, tailored to our individual needs and circumstances. None of us adheres to a particular 'school' or style of dance, except perhaps La Tati, and even she, one senses, works to her own, very personal style within the broad church that is flamenco. Some of us make use of the tools of specific disciplines – aikido, ballet, yoga – but use these in a calculated and selective way, as part of a self-maintained discipline. All of us have become teachers in order to both create a relevant context for ourselves and to share a language with others, creating new forms in the process. Most of all, we are none of us training towards some peak, as the young dancer perhaps imagines an athletic peak between, say, 25 and 30. No, we are training for life. The way we choose to move is a vital part of our whole survival. It is, in a very real way, the interface between our lives and our art. If you intend to remain a dancer until late in life, possibly until the day you die, then your physical discipline must have a meaning beyond serving the ambitions of a career.

For some of us, the practice of our dance is itself the main training: La Tati says she trains by teaching, choreographing and rehearsing. She also says she 'walks and walks'. Several of us count very basic exercise as a vital part of our training – walking, swimming, running. Some, like Julyen Hamilton, Lisa Nelson and Steve Paxton, consider labour – the tasks of growing things, digging, carrying things and generally maintaining a non-urban life-style as a major part of their training. Physical contact with the natural world seems to be an important component here – Tim Rubidge, another cast member from *Tales from the Citadel*, echoes Steve Paxton in citing the value of walking on rough, uneven terrain, as opposed to pounding flat city streets:

'Yes, your body is forever seeking out a balance. We are accustomed to be upright and try to keep a balance, whether we are walking or running, but it's fun when you are out of balance. I love being out on the fells, and so it informs my dancing, and I like that. That makes dancing less precious, not being wrapped up in silver foil; it also helps me to learn new things about the body.'[6]

Even those of us who are city dwellers often find vastly more benefit in the semi-rough terrain of, say, a London heath or wood, than in the relentless monotony of a running machine or treadmill in a gym.

Interdisciplinarity is a recurrent theme. For example, it is very interesting to know that Jane Dudley cherishes her involvement with The Group Theatre in New York in the 1930s whose work was based on Stanislavsky's methods. She says '… one of the things we were all deeply trained not to allow to happen was indicating – doing the outside instead of working from the process inside you.' Julyen Hamilton's passion for performance stemmed from his early experience acting in plays as a schoolboy; and Jacky Lansley's early training as an actress has influenced all her adult work. Philippe Priasso insists that he is a dancer but nevertheless imbues his performance with a deep sense of the dramatic relationship he can develop with his machine 'partner' in *Transports Exceptionnels*.

For all the contributors, (except Jane Dudley), the formative years were during the second half of the twentieth century. In the 1950s boundaries became blurred between painting, sculpture and performance and the individual experience of the artist became important as art became an opportunity to explore inner feelings within a changed world attempting to recover from two world wars. During the 1960s and 1970s artists, including some of our contributors, were involved in creating new forms to explore and unpick issues around gender, race and class; while the anti-Vietnam war movement produced protest art and other forms of radical and site-specific performance. This backdrop of artistic fusion, politics and diversity is the fabric of new and postmodern dance. Yet despite this, dance seems to remain vulnerable when it comes to its status as an art form – Is it art? Is it theatre? Is it community event? Are these questions relevant? Dance is really always about community wherever it takes place, as it always involves people; it cuts through all language barriers and cultures, yet this natural inclusiveness should not distract from its power as an art form, or its need to experiment and explore.

We are a fairly arbitrary selection of mature dancers; there are many experienced dance artists around the world who are breaking boundaries of age and prejudice, and making powerful and beautiful work. We believe these particular twelve journeys, however, reveal a little of that web of interconnections that is the world community of dance: a community that is not about individual stars or dance companies, but rather about dance as a way of life.

Jacky Lansley and Fergus Early, October 2010

Notes

1. Dartington Festivals: annual festivals of independent experimental dance work from the United Kingdom, the United States and Europe, organized by the US dancer and teacher Mary Fulkerson at Dartington College of the Arts in the late 1970s and 1980s.
2. X6 Dance Space (1976–81): dance studio and performance space founded by a collective of Emilyn Claid, Maedée Duprès, Fergus Early, Jacky Lansley and Mary Prestidge. An enlarged version of this collective founded New Dance magazine (1977–88). From X6 sprang Chisenhale Dance Space in the early 1980s; Chisenhale provided a base for the early development of the organisation Independent Dance (ID), established in 1990, co-directed by Gill Clarke and Fiona Millward and now based at Siobhan Davies Studios in London, UK. One of the founders of both X6 and Chisenhale, Mary Prestidge, is now part of the Liverpool Improvisation Collective, with its own studio at the Bluecoat in Liverpool, UK.
3. New Dance magazine: founded and published by X6 Dance Space in 1977, New Dance aimed to develop a language relevant to the emerging new and postmodern dance practice in the United Kingdom. It was published quarterly for 11 years.
4. Green Candle Dance Company: founded in 1987 by Fergus Early with a brief to bring dance, as practice and performance, to as wide a cross-section of the community as possible.
5. *Tales from the Citadel* (1996): Dance Umbrella Festival and UK tour. Created by Brian Bertscher, Jane Dudley, Fergus Early, Jacky Lansley and Tim Rubidge. Director Fergus Early, music Sally Davies, design Craig Givens. The piece explored the idea of a citadel as a metaphor for age – a place which holds great treasure, but which can also be a prison. See article 'The Citadel: 'A Wise Body'' by Jacky Lansley; *Performance Research* 5:1, spring 2000.
6. Quoted from personal interview with Tim Rubidge 1996. Tim is a dancer, teacher and choreographer who lives in Northumberland, United Kingdom, much of whose work has been site specific and with rural communities. He also works widely in the sphere of arts and health, often collaborating with the dance practitioner Miranda Tufnell.

Chapter 1

The Sense of Shape, the Sense of Time

Philippe Priasso

Philippe Priasso in *Transports Exceptionnels*, by Compagnie Beau Geste, 2010. Choreography and photograph: Dominique Boivin

Fergus:　When and how did you start dancing?

Philippe:　I started late, like many boys in France. I was 19 and I was taking the courses that would lead to a career in engineering, doing the preparatory classes for the *grandes écoles* – biology, higher mathematics and so on – and during these very intense classes I met a friend in the class below me who did dancing, and she said to me 'Look, to relax you, come with me, I'm doing classical ballet and maybe you'll be able to join in.' So I did this class in Lyon – just a local ballet school – and when I came out, I said 'I'm going to be a dancer!' In 1 hour it was decided. I told my parents 'This is my life, I'm going to be a dancer.' My father was driving and he gave no reaction, he just said 'Oh, I wanted to be a musician, you will be a dancer.'

Fergus:　Did you know he wanted to be a musician?

Philippe:　Well, yes. He was always playing the harmonica. He had been in the army, but he retired because he was fed up with it. But my parents said, 'We'll just pay for your accommodation – we can't manage anything more' – and of course they had already paid for my studies so far – 'but we are here, you can count on us.' So it was very simple, no objections! It was in the 1970s you see. I think it was so obvious for me that they felt they couldn't say anything, they couldn't oppose me, because I was *going* to be a dancer. Three years later, I met Alwin Nikolais,[1] when he created the Centre National de la Danse Contemporaine[2] (CNDC) in Angers – the government paid for this centre and they asked Nikolais to come and run it. He took me and he made me the dancer I am now. One day a girl asked him 'Will I be a dancer?' And he said 'No. Why? Because you asked. You don't have to ask if you *are* a dancer.' So for me, I had this certainty inside and when I saw the possibility, it was for me.

So I started in this local ballet school and within 3 months I was on stage in neo-classic and classical ballets – *The Sleeping Beauty* and so on, without knowing any better. So soon on stage! The teacher was a marvellous woman – she got very involved and when people came to her, she wanted to initiate them as soon as possible, so I was very quickly on stage, playing roles. I took part in some competitions and I did small jobs to pay my way. Then there was an audition for a workshop in Avignon with Alwin Nikolais. I passed the audition. They accepted about 40 people, including many of the best contemporary dancers in France.

Nikolais' style had already been introduced by Carolyn Carlson,[3] who had been one of his dancers. She was recruited by the Paris Opera, and so quite a number of dancers were familiar with Nikolais' style through her.

Fergus: Before she went to Paris, she taught for a while at The Place, in London, when we were there, so we knew her a bit.

Philippe: Oh yes, that's right. So when the Minister of Culture asked Nikolais to create the CNDC, he recruited dancers and, since I was doing the workshop at Avignon, he chose me to join a group of 24 dancers he would train at the CNDC. He didn't want to pick dancers who were already dancing in the contemporary dance groups, because he didn't want to 'steal' dancers from other companies. So he chose people like me that he could shape through his technique, and for me it was incredible because I learnt so much about movement at that time. After 1 year, he created the company with 10 out of the 24 dancers and I was among them. And then, when he left in 1981, I was part of the collective who created the company Beau Geste,[4] along with Dominique Boivin, who was already very well known. During the workshop, he was the star – he was an incredible performer, Nikolais adored him. Two years later Dominique took part in a workshop with Cunningham and Cage in London – they gathered choreographers and dancers from around the world …

Fergus: … I think that was the Gulbenkian Choreographic Summer School[5] …

Philippe: Yes, and both Cage and Cunningham[6] loved Dominique as well.

Jacky: How long did you work with Nikolais?

Philippe: We stayed 3 years. Nikolais was there himself for 10 weeks a year, running workshops and creating new work and the rest of the time we had master teachers visiting.

Jacky: What one knows of Nikolais' work is its strong visual language and interdisciplinarity – he was concerned with profound exploration of image and space wasn't he?

Philippe: Yes, but what was most important with Nik was that he didn't want us to know about his work, he wanted to bring us something very pure about movement – what is movement? The big four, as he called it – shape, time, space, motion – and then each day we had to improvise in lines and points, drawings, plans, time, presence in time, presence in shape, presence in space. During the 3 years we explored everything, I mean the quality of motion, poetry in motion, the sense of shape, the sense of time.

Jacky: Was this work filmed and published in some way?

Philippe: Yes. He was always writing, writing and finally, when he died, Murray [Louis],[7] his friend, gathered all the material – it was this thick – and edited it into a book which is now published in English about his technique. But to have studied with such a man – it was so simple, he was a simple man, but so precise. A point was a point, a line was a line. But you had to show that the distance between here and here is not the same as the distance between here and here (*Philippe demonstrates different lines from his eyes out into space in different directions*) – decentralization – you played with this every day. This was my training. Of course I had begun with ballet, but I was 19 and I was awkward! I could dance but … (*laughs*). It was my good fortune to meet with such a man, such an artist.

Jacky: Your background in engineering and mathematics, I suppose at some level that linked with your development as a dancer?

Philippe: Yes, of course, because for me it was very clear, it was a very scientific theory. It was not vaguely about space, for example. No, space was a value – it can be a square (*Philippe demonstrates enclosing a square space with his arms*), a projection – it was very clear. So each step was making me grow. I absorbed absolutely everything – I was new born! Nikolais said in his French that in the United States 'tout est melangé': that is to say that in the United States you couldn't find the raw material – everything was too mixed up. He wanted to train a French group because he adored French culture, the gastronomy, the wine – he was a man of the senses, someone who loved life and sensuality. He took part in the Normandy landings which explains his 'total abstract theatre', because he said the life he lived then was made up of such vivid images – light, sounds – when a bomb exploded in the night it was that that led him to his abstract theatre and even his work as a puppeteer and a musician accompanying silent films. He was a marionettist and then he began to apply the same principles to the human body – why not? It's a big machine and it comes alive!

It was because of that thinking that I grew and age has never been either a worry or an issue for me. My parents didn't question my decision, even when I was starting out, and I knew that age wouldn't be a problem when I began to work with Nikolais. At that time I knew that if I stopped, it would be because I had nothing left inside. It wouldn't be age that stopped me; it would be because I had no more life left in me. That's the special quality of these great masters of modern dance. It's extraordinary to see how the great modern and contemporary dancers after the war lived art – like painters – and I understood these things right from the start. It was important to have a good physical condition, because the training was very hard, every morning, phew! You had to learn the value of training the body, you need that. And when we started our company Beau Geste, each of us had our own individual training regimes. There were five of us and we each took responsibility for our own training. We never trained collectively. Why? Because each person had his or her own needs and because we were very interested in creation and not so interested in training! We worked collectively for 10 years. There were five of us and at the end of 10 years we gave the artistic direction back to Dominique.[8] By 1991 there were three of us left: we are an artistic team, where each of us has a role.

Fergus: Who is the third person?

Philippe: It's Christine Erbé. She, Dominique and I all remained from the original company. The projects were always linked one to another and when there were low points we re-connected with each other and shared ideas, because we had time – we weren't touring any more. That was in the late 1980s and early 1990s and it was a moment when we could refuel ourselves, because we had a lot of time. That time allowed us to launch several projects which really found their audience. The training had to follow the work. Christine decided not to continue dancing for personal and physical reasons but Dominique is 57, and still dances on stage.

Jacky: We wanted to ask you about the core processes of your company, Beau Geste, and you've already begun to do that. But perhaps you would like to say more.

Philippe: When we left the CNDC in 1981, we formed a group, because we couldn't imagine putting ourselves at the service of other choreographers. We had been formed as dancers, teachers and choreographers. So, we were a group of seven for 1 year and then five for the next 10 years – two men, three women – and we were a collective. At one point the group pieces were truly collective: eight counts for one dancer, eight counts for the next and so on. It was incredible! All the choreography came out of an assemblage of 'cells' of eight counts by each of the five dancers. It had an incredible unity. I remember the choreography very well. We have it on film. We recorded everything on film right from the start – now it's all on DVD – we have an enormous bank of material. I remember that Nik, before he left the CNDC said to us 'You're ready to make improvised pieces.'

Fergus: So did you give improvised performances?

Philippe: Yes, we did; after this period of collective choreography, which followed every beat of the music exactly, we improvised everything! We worked for 3 months on improvisation around specific themes: masculinity, femininity, meetings and so on, but there was no order. It corresponded to the music, which was live playing of records on a record player, in chance-determined order. There were three women's costumes and two men's and we changed on stage. I could find myself dressed as a man or a woman and didn't know at what moment anything would happen. It was called *Venus et les toutous* – 'Venus and the doggies' – we had the body of an airplane on stage and it was like a landing strip with lights all round and a large white carpet. We came out of the plane. After that, we decided to 'fix' the improvisations; but what we also decided was to take all the music and sing it and play it ourselves. None of us was a musician! So we stayed in a cellar for 20 days and we tried to reproduce all these records – there were Stray Cats, Holiday by the Bee Gees and James Brown's Sex Machine – we made incredible versions of them! And then we used this music.

Jacky: And did it work?

Philippe: Yes. It was called *Désir désir*. It was the desire to do something one didn't know how to do. It was imperative at that moment that things were fixed, set. We set the choreography. But we were working on what we called 'mouvement sale'.

Philippe Priasso in *Blême Aurore* (*Pale Dawn*), by Compagnie Beau Geste. Choreography and photograph: Dominique Boivin

Fergus: What did that mean?

Philippe: Dirty movement, movement that isn't clean, isn't elegant, broken movement, really dirty movement. In fact people would ask us 'Do you really know how to dance?' That was fine by us! After that, we collaborated with another collective which also came out of the CNDC – Lolita – in order to create a revue, complete with sequins, and we asked Christian Lacroix, the costume designer, to create the costumes. We went to the Bataclan[9] in Paris and we created the revue and it was re-mounted the following year with different dancers. So these were the adventures we were having. Then each of us got involved with our personal lives and other relationships. Geographically, we weren't any longer together. It was very difficult to function – there were two of us in Paris, three in Rouen. So it was decided in 1991 to re-form the group: we gave the direction to Dominique Boivin and formed an artistic team of three.

Fergus: Did the company receive state subsidy?

Philippe: The company arrived at a good moment. François Mitterrand was elected in 1981.[10] So one was present at the emergence of a cultural world in France. That's not to say that there wasn't some money around before that – the proof of that is that the CNDC was actually created under a government of the right – I was paid to be a student at the CNDC, just to learn, I earned more than the minimum wage for 3 years. And when I joined the company I earned twice as much.

Jacky: The French government really supported dance.

Philippe: Yes, even before François Mitterrand, because all those companies emerged in the 1970s. Then in the 1980s, it exploded, because Mitterrand came in with Jack Lang as Minister of Culture[11] and there was even more money.

Jacky: In the UK there was also a big explosion of dance in the 1970s, but in the 1980s the government didn't support it and a lot of interesting people and groups didn't flourish, because the government failed to do what the French did, which seemed to be extraordinary.

Philippe: It was incredible. For Beau Geste's first 2 years we were on unemployment benefit, then when we had money we could pay everybody, then we were unemployed again and so on. After that, we received subsidies from the government, the region and also the département – so you see there were a lot of sources of money. Of course, I have observed over 30 years that sometimes money is not always good; it's sometimes not well spent! I'm not saying it was too much. Art has need of means, but there can be a contradiction between on the one hand energizing the things that just need some help and on the other of continuing to give money and give money, because that just produces institutions, structures that are ossified. Anyway, it was a time of great financial support, and really, thank you! Because we benefited greatly from it. There was a law, called the Statut d'Intermittent du Spectacle: in France, if you gave 42 performances in a year, you could claim a daily sum of money for all the time you weren't performing, and this could be enough to live comfortably. I benefited from this statute for several years at the end of the 1980s and the beginning of the 1990s, and we lived well. The law still exists, though it's been modified, and it is very, very advantageous.

Fergus: And you just have to do 42 performances?

Philippe: Yes, 42 – and one can arrange that in lots of ways.

Jacky: The Beau Geste studio is in a rural situation, isn't it? A lot of the artists we have spoken to are based in independent studios, sometimes rural, sometimes urban. Is it important to you where you are?

Philippe: First we worked in different spaces, where people wanted the company, but when we finally settled it was in a town in Normandy called Val de Reuil and we just moved into a ruined barn which used to house sheep and goats – I adored it! I adored this space, because we were free to do what we wanted, we weren't disturbed, we had a huge amount of time – it was a special moment. Then we decided to ask the local council if we could build a studio on an island. It had to be passed by the various authorities and Jack Lang asked for it to be designed by a Japanese architect, Kasutoshi Morita. It was on an island formed by two branches of the river Eure. So it is in the middle of nature, the doors open out onto a view of the river, it's a beautiful building. It was built in 1996 and inaugurated in 1997. We worked with the architect, stone by stone. Unfortunately, he didn't sign off the building, because he didn't recognize it as his work. He wanted a very high standard of work, like a modern Japanese building, but there wasn't enough money for this from the municipality, which, together with the regional government, was paying for the construction. And there weren't the artisans who could live up to the aesthetic demands he was making on them. So we found ourselves with a building we had to complete. But we weren't foremen, so it was hard. Anyway, now we had a building and what we wanted was the maximum space for dance.

So we have a dance floor of 150 square metres and two huge 10 metre doors which open and can transform the space into an outdoor theatre. And at the other end, screens which open onto a view of the river. It's a space for us, but from time to time we also allow it to be used by other companies in the region or sometimes international companies. It's a recognition, even if one doesn't have funds to help, of how difficult it is for dancers to find space to work in, and so we feel a duty to help. The space is one which allows artists to work. There is also a small flat in the town, where people can stay. It's a big responsibility, because we are also touring, doing up to 200 performances a year. It takes a lot of time to maintain it. But it is in open countryside, with rabbits – too many rabbits! – a cat which eats the rabbits, a fox and so on. Choreographers adore the space, because they can totally immerse themselves in the work. Unfortunately, the studio has been broken into three times and so we have had to take away the big opening doors.

Fergus: So how do you feel now, as a dancer and as a physical being, in comparison to how you felt 30 years ago? What's the difference?

Philippe: The difference is the maturity, of the body, but also of the mind. Because as you grow older, you begin to relax and to get back to a simplicity of execution of movement. You expend less energy, you measure it more carefully. I've never been in better shape than I am now, because this performance [*Transports Exceptionnels*] and the machine I work with make enormous demands on the body. Before I began working with the machine, I was on form, but when I began, I became like a block of concrete, I felt really bad – all the improvising with the machine and all the shows made me feel physically bad. Now I get aches and pains of course – it's my iron partner that gives me those: when she caresses me, it hurts! – but I've learnt how to ration my energy in a way I never could before. It's risky for sure, because it can be dangerous. But only a dancer could perform this piece. A dancer is disciplined, exacting, rigorous. Sometimes someone says to me 'Why don't you get someone to take your place, an acrobat, for example?' I say, just try it and you'll see.

I don't think I've ever felt better in my body than I do now. There are some aches in the morning, sure, but if you pay attention to them, they go. Sometimes I train with the machine, because I haven't the time to train myself. I think that a mature dancer is training in the street, just walking. I'm dancing in the street when I'm walking. Of course there are things I have to do. I have to do 100 push-ups, because when I stand on my hands I want the line to be perfect. When the machine puts me on my hands, I don't want to struggle, I just want to *be*, you know what I mean? So, if I want to *be*, I need the means, I need to be free during the performance. It's really the *being* that is called upon during the performance. It's a state that you can only attain with maturity, I think. In youth – you can balance, you can throw yourself against the walls, you can roll on the floor – and that's fine, it's beautiful, it's magnificent and I love to see it, but one learns to pace oneself, to work just so, to understand what the meaning of a form is, what it means to an audience. There is obviously a bodily transition. At one time in my life I was concerned with physical development of the body – I was concerned with muscularity. We had a project, *Carmen*, and I was playing Don José and the idea was to have a masculinity that also embraced fragility. So, I appeared very sculpted and I had to start standing on my hands – I had never done this and I had no idea how to hold myself, so when we started I said, 'I'll never do that, it's impossible.' But I went to a famous gymnastics team in Normandy and learned how to do it. But even when you've learned and have done it a thousand times in rehearsal, it's a different matter to do it on stage in front of an audience, in front of 3,000 people!

I've never wanted to let go the things I have acquired. As you get older, you continue to train; until now, there's no problem but it's because one has practised and practised over such a long period. That's why I was able to tackle this work with the machine. One day as we were coming back from an event in Strasbourg which used a digger, though no dancer, Dominique said to me, 'We'll rent a digger and you can work with it, because you have the physical and mental strength to do it.' I learned a lot about mental processes with this piece, because in all weathers, whether it rains, whether the wind is blowing, you've got to be right there.

Fergus: Isn't it dangerous in the rain?

Philippe: It's always dangerous, but I decided that it all happened in my head and that when the mind is on top of things, it's amazing what the body can discover, even during the show. There are certainly risks, but a dancer's strength, a dancer's intelligence is extraordinary – and I'm not talking about myself – but of dancers in general.

Jacky: Yes, the alertness, the adaptability, those skills. And what you're saying is that you have more now than when you were younger.

Philippe: Yes, much more. That's maturity. You have the knowledge, the *body* has the knowledge.

Jacky: Our book is called *The Wise Body*.

Philippe: Oh yes, it's true, it is a form of wisdom, for sure. We find a wisdom inside us which leads us and helps us adapt to all conditions, particularly an outdoor piece where it might rain, it might blow or even be below zero temperatures – I'm never cold, because there's such an intensity during the performance. In your mind you have so many strengths that you can develop.

Fergus: And your driver?

Philippe: He's our lighting designer, Eric Lamy. One time I performed in front of 200 digger drivers. The boss was the only one who had seen the piece before and he said 'I want them to see this.' At the end, the drivers said 'We wouldn't do this – it's much too dangerous, too much responsibility'. Of course you can drive it, it's very easy to drive, but to measure exactly the energy needed on the controls, to combine the movements without the bucket suddenly stopping – BAF! – like that, when I'm in the bucket – that can be really dangerous, it really needs extreme attention. Eric is someone who understands a dancer's body. What he does is like a caress.

Fergus: Had he driven a digger before?

Philippe: No. He had to take two tests, one for 5–10 tonnes and one for 10–30 tonnes. Because we use all sizes from 5 or 6 tonnes up to 30 tonnes.

Fergus: How big is the one you are using here in Manchester?

Philippe: 7 tonnes.

Jacky: This is obviously a piece that has caught the imagination of many, many people, it's a dance that people really want to see and I was just thinking about what are the main metaphors, because even though you are talking about strength, focus, power, actually the image is one of total vulnerability in contrast to this massive, hefty machine. It's that dialogue, isn't it – you, the human being, are so vulnerable?

Philippe: You see, I've received so many reactions after the show. For me the total experience is before, during and after the show – very much after. For example, yesterday, in Bury, we were in a commercial centre that had only been open 1 week, a pedestrianized shopping centre, and this guy came up at the end and said 'I've been working on building the centre and it's amazing to see such poetry in this place.' In the centre of Sao Paulo, in Brazil, at the end of the last performance – there were millions of people, because it was the 'White Night Festival'[12] – there was a guy, he had his wife and two children with him and he had almost no teeth, he was in tears and he just wanted to hug me. It's incredible; we can't know what is going on for people. I don't want to know, because each person will have their own story. They have their own backgrounds and they can imagine what they want. But you know, it has rejuvenated me. It's fed me so much. Even if it had to end tomorrow – what an adventure! I've never known anything like it.

Fergus: You don't get tired of doing it?

Philippe: No, it can't get boring, because each show is different. Each machine is different, the context is different, the architecture. You might be dancing in front of Rheims Cathedral, right in front of its amazing facade, or the cathedral in Santiago de Compostela as I was only a month ago, or Chartres – it's incredible! Sometimes it's a shock, but what a gift. Thank you, Dominique!

Jacky: Dominique who created the piece?

Philippe: Yes, he created the piece. He had the idea. Of course all three of us had a say, because later Christine came and said 'You could use this music here' and so on and afterwards I changed a lot of his choreography – we always work together. But he had the idea of doing something tender, not a fight, not the usual 'man against machine'.

Fergus: No, it's like a love affair.

Philippe: Yes, so as a performer you have to persuade the audience that it's true. That's why I work a lot with focus, thanks to Nikolais, to give intention to the machine. In fact to use everything that's at my disposal as a theatrical skill. I'm not an actor, I'm a dancer and it's really a dancer who does that. I'm not an acrobat either. I'm a dancer.

Fergus: It makes me think of something you talk about a lot, Jacky, which is the drama of the object.

Philippe Priasso in *Transports Exceptionnels*, by Compagnie Beau Geste, 2010. Choreography and photograph: Dominique Boivin

Philippe: Yes, because we have this faculty of anthropomorphism: that is, transferring life to an inanimate object. That way the object can really become magnificent. How many times have people said to me 'I'm in love with that digger!'

Jacky: So what are your physical disciplines?

Philippe: Nikolais' theoretical training is very present. I know his floor barre and his warm-up, I can teach his 'displacements' and his body evolution in workshops. But I have already integrated the principles of decentralization, of precision into my training, so I concentrate specifically on the muscles, as I need to do for a very demanding performance task. So I use stretching and very repetitive physical exercises.

Fergus: Is the stretching yoga-based?

Philippe: No, because I haven't studied yoga, but I feel inside that it could be very 'yoga', because although in life I am someone who travels a lot, on stage everything becomes very calm and I know that it is only the structure of the body which allows that to happen. When you're solid on your legs, when you're solid in your support, you can tackle anything. I work very much with the idea of stability and of the connection between the psyche and the body. And always not to cheat, when I look, when I place a hand, when I lie down, it's my being, it's a matter of how to be in a state of freedom and not fabricate, not act. My physical training is a bit basic, but at root it's completely impregnated with this philosophy. They may be very repetitive movements, but even if they are repetitive, I'll make sure I finish in a state of relaxation and with muscles that are not strained. I have to get myself ready for a very specific piece. It's strange, the relationship which I have now with our studio, our space. I hardly go there at all. I'm always on the road, so the smallest space – a hotel room – has to become a rehearsal room; the street can become a rehearsal room, a warm-up space. I remember in Marrakesh, in Morocco, in the Djemaa el Fna Square with minarets all round, there was an enormous digger and I found a little corner and warmed up among all the snake charmers and story tellers! It's really a sacred responsibility, I feel very responsible. So I rarely drink alcohol, I have a life regime that is at the service of this piece. And that's maturity, too. When I was young, I couldn't have lived like that, I didn't want to. But now I don't want to destroy the instrument which allows me to do the thing that nourishes me. So I keep within limits, I live a very moderate life. And even if I don't feel an enormous difference, I know that if I exceed my limits, it would collapse!

Jacky: We've talked about your emotional development as an artist and dancer and the psychological journey to find that discipline of being that involves the whole self. I guess over the 30 years it's also about dealing with personal issues.

Philippe: I quit my studies which could have led to a career as an engineer, which my parents were counting on. It was my own personal demand which said 'I choose this, but it's going to be for life. It's not a whim. It's a very serious decision.' I think that's probably why my parents didn't say anything: even if friends said 'Oh it's not possible, he's dropped out of his engineering career, what's he going to do when he's 40, he won't be able to dance anymore.' I think my parents said 'No, you're mistaken.'

Fergus: And what do they think of you now? Are they proud of you?

Philippe: Of course! They've always come to everything. This piece with the digger and the risks I take make it hard for my mother. Once I was performing on Reunion Island, near South Africa, and everybody in the audience was sitting, except one person – my mother – she was standing and she was so tense!

Fergus: Now the final question; for you, how important is dance?

Philippe: Dance has impregnated my life. Even if I stopped dancing, I would still be a dancer. It's so much a way to preserve my space for life, to maintain my relations and my way of being with others. It's something which is physically, organically, psychically health-giving. I am a dancer. Even if I stopped in 2 years – because one never knows what's going to happen – if I ran out of talent or whatever, even then, it wouldn't change what is inside me, that'll be there forever. I don't frequent the 'dance world'. I never have. Why? It's as if I already had the nourishment I needed. I have good relations with many people in dance, but I've never thought of myself as belonging to a particular milieu. Even when I was a kid, I didn't like playing football, I didn't want to belong to a scene that would restrict me. So why go back into a place which I see as rigid and fixed? So I've lived the dance in a very free way. But I've been protected by a group – I could live that way because I've been protected. We gave ourselves the conditions for the group to exist. Because we were such different personalities, I've been enriched by these personalities and then we also sought out other artists and brought them to us. I don't know why, maybe through timidity, but I've always wanted to be the one to choose my own contaminations and my own models. I know that one is shaped; I know that one chooses the models, one is formed by imitation – you copy, you copy, you copy – but I wanted to choose *who* I imitated, I didn't want to enter a world of conformist imitation. I felt that very, very early on. I wanted to learn movement, because that seemed to be something that had to be done. And with Nikolais I had extraordinary luck, I think if I hadn't met him I would have stopped. Because in fact, just before the workshop in Avignon, I did a classical dance workshop for 3 weeks in Troyes. I was so innocent, so naive that I was completely flattened. I was nothing, nothing. I was also very angry – it was a workshop organized by the Conservatoire de Paris, so it was attended by students of the Conservatoire, with teachers from Paris. I was paying and I was very disappointed. I was thinking 'Oh my God, what have I done? This is no good.' The dancers were very good, but the principal teacher was awful. Straight after that I took my suitcase and went to Avignon and there I said 'Wow!' It was very good luck.

I didn't learn dance through a particular style, because Nikolais taught an analysis of movement; he talked to us about what form is; one learnt about body shape, the sense of sculpture – you learn a lot, you gained a consciousness of the totality; it was also an aesthetic technique. Nikolais was profoundly generous and gave and gave to a kid like me who was *nothing*. He was so curious – he wanted to see what was going to happen. It was wonderful to see what pleasure he took in seeing people transform.

Fergus: It was a special moment for him too, I suspect.

Philippe: Yes, very special. We stayed in contact right up to his death. Then there were homages from all the dancers who had worked with him. If I stopped dancing tomorrow, I'd still be fed by what I learned from him. It was a moment in my life when I really made a choice. *The* choice. Because you don't make 50 such choices. And after that you understand a little more about yourself. You begin to understand yourself after this meeting with dance. So now it's part of me, it's inside.

Fergus: And how important is dance for the world?

Philippe: For the world itself, I think dance is nothing. Of course now I have travelled a lot and I've seen a lot of dancers and choreographers in Japan, the United States, Brazil, South Africa, Morocco, Israel; you meet all these people and I say to myself 'The dancers are the best.' They are people who are in their bodies; they have an incredible will and discipline.

Fergus: That's not nothing!

Philippe: No, of course it's not nothing. For me it's enormous, but I meant that for the whole world, well people hardly know that dance exists…

Fergus: But if they knew …

Philippe: Yes! If they knew! Everywhere we go in the world – we were in Mexico last week – you can see dancers. You don't have such richness in theatre, dancers have a connection.

Jacky: A global network …

Philippe: Korea, Japan, Australia, New Zealand, China, it's so tiny, but we are all connected. I think dancers are the best.

Manchester, UK, 24 July 2010

Notes

1. Alwin Nikolais (1910–93): US choreographer, composer and designer, known for his 'total theatre' that integrated these elements. In 1951 he formed the Nikolais Dance Theater to present his productions of integrated motion, sound, shape and colour. Nikolais directed the Centre for

Contemporary Dance in Angers, France (1979–81). In 1989 his company merged with another to form the Nikolais and Murray Louis Dance Company.

2. Le Centre National de Danse Contemporaine: the National Centre of Contemporary Dance in Angers was the first of a network of National Choreographic Centres set up around France to promote the practice of dance and provide bases for professional companies to create and present work as well as teach and promote dance of a high standard in the French regions.

3. Carolyn Carlson: US dancer and choreographer who was a leading dancer with the Alwin Nikolais dance company. She was leading choreographer at the Paris Opera Ballet and since 2004 has been Artistic Director of the National Choreographic Centre of Roubaix Nord-Pas de Calais.

4. Beau Geste: French contemporary dance company, Artistic Director Dominique Boivin and dance artists Philippe Priasso and Christine Erbé, based in Val de Reuil, Normandy, France.

5. The Gulbenkian Choreographic Summer School (later the International Course for Professional Choreographers and Composers) brought together choreographers, composers, dancers and musicians for an intensive period of research and collaboration. From the mid 1970s to the mid 1990s it was held annually and directed by different artists.

6. John Cage (1912–92) composer, artist and poet and Merce Cunningham (1919–2009) choreographer: long-term collaborators in creating some of the most influential American avant garde dance and music of the twentieth century.

7. Murray Louis: Nikolais' long-term collaborator and principal dancer, he lives and works in New York and has made 2 influential film series: *Dance as an Art Form* and *The World of Alwin Nikolais*.

8. Dominique Boivin: dancer, choreographer, one of the original founders of Beau Geste and its Artistic Director.

9. Le Bataclan: cabaret and concert hall in Paris.

10. François Mitterrand: Socialist French President; the 21st President of the French Republic, served from 1981 until 1995.

11. Jack Lang: French Minister of Culture (1981–86 and 1991–92); hugely increased state subsidy to arts and culture.

12. White Night Festival in Sao Paulo, Brazil, also known as the Virada Cultural, is an annual 24-hour city-wide festival of events, many in the streets.

Chapter 2

Growing New Patterns from a New Imagination

Lisa Nelson

Lisa Nelson leading a Tuning Score workshop at Estudio Nova Dança, Saõ Paulo, Brazil, 2006. Photograph: Gil Grossi

Jacky: What is your earliest memory of dance? Earliest positive memory?

Lisa: I think when I was about 3 I went to a dance class – which is so strange – to think that a dance class is probably my earliest memory of dance. The 'dance' was prancing around mimicking the story of the ugly duckling to a record. It's a vivid memory. I remember the dance studio in which it happened. I remember that it was something that was social because it was a group of people, so that value was part of what dancing was. I know I enjoyed it. Where I grew up in Queens, New York, there wasn't really any dancing around me except the marching bands that would occasionally come through the neighbourhood, with black men wearing green marching costumes. It was incredible colour to see and as they were marching, they were also playing instruments and that fascinated me – the rhythm and the colour. It's possible that I was attracted to it because of the music. I would not separate my early experiences from music.

Jacky: So already dance is social and it involves music and musicians?

Lisa: Right, early on.

Jacky: What made you decide to become a professional dancer?

Lisa: When I was 5 or 6 I started formally taking classes with a teacher, Nadya Romanoff Abeles, who had a children's dance company. We made our own dances and this was really my foundation because I love making dances. So I was very active making dances and I would choose music and I would make some kind of format for myself. By the time I was 9 or 10, I was making the dances to silence and then looking for music afterwards.

Jacky: So it was already quite a sophisticated process? And can you remember what kind of movement, and what your formats were?

Lisa: Well the first dance I made was called 'Paramesium' and the movement I think was very small and amorphous. I don't really remember the movement but I remember the dance, and I don't think that it had any music.

Jacky: And did you perform?

Lisa: We made and performed the dances. Nadya was a very colourful character who also taught us the history of ballet and the history of jazz. So I had a very early introduction to some fantastic music and an understanding of the history of ballet – the personalities, the styles – somehow that was all part of what modern dance was. I was aware that I was good at it and that I liked it. I went to dance classes and rehearsals once a week and we travelled from community centre to community centre with our show. That was very early, and I'm still doing that. My mother was very supportive, she got me to the dance class every week and once when I didn't want to go to a rehearsal she chased me around until I went. When I was 11 it was suggested that I go to study dance formally and I got into Juilliard[1] Preparatory Division in Manhattan. Everything shifted then. I danced all day on Saturdays and studied Ballet, Graham and music theory and I was invited into the composition class. Most of the other students were older in the composition class. When I auditioned I remember the improvising pianist asked 'do you want fast music or slow music?' I don't know which one I said, but if I said 'slow' I danced fast and if I said 'fast' I danced slow, and I remember Pearl Lang,[2] who was auditioning me, thought that was a bit advanced and invited me into her class. Because I wasn't following the music, something was very deliberate. I have to mention that I also studied piano and shifted to classical guitar when I was 12, so I was deeply involved with music.

At my second class, Pearl asked me to repeat a dance and although I thought I did, she said I didn't. I was totally shocked and she told me I had to remember my movements. So I worked out a strategy for remembering movements.

Jacky: And you thought you had repeated the dance?

Lisa: Well, I was sure it was the same dance. I choreographed only solos and at one point she asked us to choreograph a duet or a trio, and I tried and it didn't agree with me. I got a little ruined during that period because at the end, at sixteen, I think I had lost my more personal movement, I was more influenced by technique and I think I was doing less interesting movement than I had during the earlier years.

Jacky: You were doing what sort of movement? Graham?

Lisa: Yes and ballet, and I had to get rid of them later, which wasn't hard because I knew what had been there before. I remember thinking about how to continue dancing when I was through with high school – whether to go to a conservatory, like Juilliard, which I didn't want to do, or to become a 'choreographer'; but even as I thought it, I was asking the question – what the hell is a choreographer? I remember thinking that I was not really sure, but I made a decision to go to Bennington College,[3] a liberal arts college which took a creative approach to dance, from where things shifted quite a bit.

Jacky: So that was the main intention, to choreograph? Somehow it got separate from being a dancer?

Lisa: Well, I knew I didn't want to be in someone's company, but I wanted to continue to perform. Performing was already habitual; in the earlier years it was a great pleasure and I got very high. Though it became a struggle on and off over the years. I would make my dances, sketching out the shape of things, but they weren't going to really live until I was performing them.

Jacky: You were working visually with yourself?

Lisa: A little bit. I would make the dances in my living room, which was very small with furniture, and there was a window in which I could see my reflection. I would work at night, but I could only see my reflection from the waist up.

Jacky: You had an interest in the sculptural qualities of movement?

Lisa: I had an interest in what it looked like, so I wasn't simply making the dance from an internal place. I changed movements based on that window image. I was crafting both from the outside and the inside, and also accumulating a dance, one movement after another, but I would always find a place for the movements I was interested in if the order didn't seem right.

Jacky: Given that you started that very integrated choreographic process so young, which I think is very unusual, what do you think it has given you?

Lisa: Well, for one thing, habit. It was really important that I had a habit, a making- habit with dancing.

When I was 24, in 1973, I quit dancing, which was a huge discovery because I had been dancing all my life. I didn't know whether I would ever start again.

Jacky: And how long was that for?

Lisa: It turned into being maybe 3 years. To come back, I felt like I really needed to make a commitment as an adult to something that I had done more or less without question since I was a child. For about half a year before I stopped, I had started walking out of performances, and was having a hard time performing.

Jacky: You were improvising exits?

Lisa: Yes and not really knowing that I wasn't going to return but finding myself unable to return to the space, and that was the beginning of wondering what I was doing. There were a lot of things happening at once; I had gained a lot of weight, my body was really uncomfortable, so it was because of both the loss of contact with my physicality and the loss of contact with what I was working on that I started walking out of performances.

When I was 27, I felt I started from the beginning for the first time and was looking for some anatomical information that I could support my teaching with. My teaching up until then was concerned with how one learns, because I didn't feel that I had any technical information to share. I didn't then know of a technical training that could look at your own organization and help maximize it rather than change your organization to fit some other person's idea about what you should be doing with your body. Though I had bumped into release technique[4] the year before I quit, it didn't appeal to me. Release technique seemed to be focused on muscle and skeletal systems and although I knew it wasn't designed towards a particular style of movement, somehow I couldn't relate to muscles and skeleton as the source of dancing, even though I certainly had plenty of muscle aches and pains. Although Graham crafted a technique that came from the centre, relating to eastern philosophies of movement, it too just didn't fit my body very well.

Anyway, I had started to dance again around 1976 and I had been looking for a physiology to study when I bumped into Bonnie Bainbridge Cohen and Body-Mind Centering.[5] In 1977 Steve Paxton[6] and I were doing duet performances with solo dancing and some contact, and Bonnie came to see our show and invited us over for dinner and gave us a review on our brain function, which was hilarious and fascinating. After this meeting, I decided to go to study with Bonnie. I related well to her experiential study of anatomy which went beyond muscles and skeleton, and the learning process that she was involved in matched my learning process. Bonnie's work was very important because I immediately thought I could identify the physical source of my own dancing, which was from the organs. I had a very active torso – who knows what I was ever doing with my arms and legs – and I was and am very active in the organs and in the eyes. That gave me a lot of material to explore, since her system is so global, everything is interlaced. One way I used her work was to try to connect my upper and lower body. I had an extreme upper/lower body split which made me a very bad gymnast, for one thing. So I had a clear technical need for 'improving' my instrument, and practicing contact improvisation, which I thought of as a fantastic diagnostic dance form that provided feedback on the integration of my upper and lower limbs into my centre. The split slowly came together through working with glands and organs, mostly through breathing and visualizing anatomical structures.

Jacky: How did you first encounter contact improvisation?

Lisa: I first saw it on video in 1972 shortly after its first performances. I had returned to Bennington to teach dance there and met Steve who'd been teaching there for the preceding half-year and was developing contact with some of the students. Contact totally blew me away. My improvisational work up to then was also based on communication and touch was not alien.

And Contact was fantastic because it was a self-teaching form. That appealed to me because my main interest in teaching was about how one learns. In my dance classes I had devised ways in which everyone was teaching each other and here was a form that taught itself, and that was fabulously interesting to me. So the reflexes being the teacher and the movement being the teacher in Steve's formulation of contact was a complete eureka.

What also intrigued me was the idea that there were images that you could *follow* rather than impose onto your intention. Contact was so clear – you just fell and you followed what happened; you didn't just touch someone, you leaned on them, and you followed the weight.

Jacky: There is a strong sense of emotional embodiment in your work. Can you talk about this?

Lisa: When I was working with Daniel Nagrin's[7] improvisation company, the Workgroup, in '71 and '72 in New York, which based its structures on Joseph Chaikin's Open Theatre[8] exercises of interaction and emotional conflict, I found no physical underpinning for the work. When he offered us imagery, like 'I am not an animal, I am a human being,' or images that were conflictual or emotional images, I couldn't find a way to work with them, they just didn't translate for me into movement. So I was aware that I wasn't very good working with metaphorical images. My strategy was to start moving and find something that was going on in my body and work from that. When I created images for myself, they came from my physical circumstance and if I had to describe them to somebody I would usually describe them with a language of limitation like 'I can't move my arm' or 'my hand is connected to my breast' and I would explore whatever movement came out of that. I created localized physical limitations and then let the body deal with it.

A year or so earlier, I had taken some classes with Judith Dunn who was an early improvisational artist who taught at Bennington and had been a Cunningham dancer and, like Steve, was associated with the Judson Dance Theater[9] (she was married to Robert Dunn[10] who taught the composition classes that led to Judson). One day, in the middle of one of her improv sessions she handed me a pair of shoes and said, 'you are doing so much with your hands, why don't you just hold these shoes?' and I held the shoes and what happened was so obvious and profound. I held the shoes throughout the session but I could tell that it didn't change what I was doing and that I was still very hand-orientated. So holding the shoes as a 'limitation' on my movement didn't get to the root of anything about my movement or where it was coming from; its rhythmic and energetic organization didn't change at all. I realized I needed some new sources to study movement.

Jacky: Just to clarify – when you were given the limitation of the shoes but were continuing to work the same way, was that about a sense of not being able to focus and direct – there was some kind of reflexive work going on in the hands that you wanted to understand? Was there pleasure in the work with the hands?

Lisa: Now I understand a lot more. My hands and my eyes – both are extremities and quick as lightning – were and are still a very central part of my body thinking. They're both a source of where the movement comes from and my antennae – the way I reach into and support myself in the world; and my feet also, I was very feety. At the time of the hand thing, I wasn't thinking about my hands, I wasn't shaping them. My hands were rather eclectic. I was never using them gesturally as many people do. In a way they were disconnected from my body and awareness. I was in pieces. The hands were a manifestation of an energetic layer of my movement source. The same with my eyes, though my eyes are reflectors of my attention and intention, I've come to learn they're more often the initiators and stabilizers of my movement. My eyes have been a very active part of my dancing since I was very little, but I wasn't attending to them at all, neither was I attending to my hands, but I did see that putting something at the ends of my body, the shoes, didn't change my source which was really energetic and organic; it didn't change my basic pattern at that point. That's all I knew.

Jacky: So you discovered Contact?

Lisa: When I discovered Contact, it was very restful as a technique for moving improvisationally – but for me it was also about *following* and, at that point, gave me an opportunity to let go of a lot of excess movement which was irrelevant to the contact interactions. There were two things that weren't that appealing: One – I just wasn't much of an athlete or gymnast and didn't love rolling; it never really appealed to me. I was intrigued with learning how to use my own weight but wasn't that interested in carrying people around. Two – because I was small, people liked to lift me and throw me around and I didn't enjoy that. I didn't like it politically that the small women were thrown around. Even though contact gave you the opportunity to be on the bottom as much as on the top, my shoulders didn't really accommodate big people. I could lift people but it wasn't a pleasure, and my politics weren't that strong that I felt like I had to prove something by carrying men on my shoulders. I was fascinated by how the form of the dance came naturally out of the technique. I loved watching it and I loved the reflex play, particularly when I was going fast. I found my reflexes very titillated and because I didn't like to roll that much I tended to save myself on my feet – I had a low centre of gravity – right before hitting the ground with my body. I was constantly surprised how ingenious my body was that I could be in a flying fall and find my feet.

But that was beside the point. I also didn't want to practise rolling, I didn't want to learn new formal movement patterns. I was done with formal techniques. I had stopped studying them when I was 18 or 19, and when I stopped dancing at 24 I wanted to let some of my muscle patterns atrophy; disuse seemed like the fastest way to get rid of pointed toes and stuff like that – and it did happen over time. That was a consequence of quitting, I was being very physical, working on the farm, but I was not pointing my toes. I mean working on the farm you just don't point your toes! So those things slowly atrophied, which was fine, and when I started dancing again, I just didn't want to acquire another habitual movement pattern, like rolling. Like the techniques I practised when I was younger – Graham and ballet, I was good enough to be asked to join someone's company, but I didn't *feel* good at it. It was painful, it was alien to my body. I put a lot of dancing into my technical training, so I suppose it looked OK but I didn't always enjoy it and I didn't want to change my body to learn another one. I could see that the contact technique as it was developing with Steve and Nancy Stark Smith[11] and Danny Lepkoff,[12] who were all fabulous gymnasts, had an inclination towards a language of movement which wasn't mine.

But those were very conscious choices I was able to make and I was determined to learn the basics of contact which was through work with the weight. I had studied T'ai Chi when I was 19 in New York, realizing that was my ticket to getting grounded. Contact clearly was also my way to learn about the weight going down, but I wanted to learn it in my own structure with my own movement. However, working with carrying and lifting people was very important in getting the feedback I needed to get the weight to flow down through my skeleton, so I couldn't discard the form of the practice.

Jacky: Can we turn to your work with video?

Lisa: That was serendipitous. When I stopped dancing in 1974, I picked up a video camera because it was there and discovered how much my sense of vision was my source of moving and connected to my choreographic urge. Earlier on, my sources for my improvisational dances and collaborations weren't about the details of movement, but more about relationship either to my environment or to other people, it was about communication. Little by little I learnt about video through teaching it to the students at Bennington where I had been teaching dance. For a while I was just videoing everything around and learning how to see and edit. I was running a community cable TV station in the rural town near where I lived and programming everything, anything – farms, pigs, dance, town meetings, high school theatre, everything around.

I wasn't a natural at all with the camera. I had never touched a camera in my life before picking up the video camera, so I really was learning from scratch. Video is an instant feedback system, much like contact is in movement. You shot and you looked right back at it and you could remember what you were thinking while shooting and have a dialogue with your own output/input. So it was a learning machine and it fit right into my passion with teaching about how you learn.

I was very bad at being pre-intentional with my looking: I didn't know what the frame was offering me and didn't know the conventions. I followed my nose. But I would see afterwards what got framed, and I became aware of my own patterns of organizing what I was looking at. I was looking through the camera with one eye while the other eye was closed and the camera was part of my head, so my whole body was following my interest. In a sense, the image was always *in* my body which had to shape itself in a certain way to capture the image. I was becoming a container for my tool which was the camera itself – my body was an extension of the camera. With each successive zoom in, your movement changes. You become like the tail of the snake and your movement is completely connected to what you are framing. I did all kinds of experiments in my learning – including not looking through the camera but using it as a part of my body, and doing 'blind' work.

Jacky: Here, now, your eyes are very enlivened but yet they are also resting.

Lisa: Now I am so different with my eyes. They feel so calm now; I lost my far vision in my early 30s. Looking in the viewfinder at a fixed distance, for so many years, I slowly hurt my eyes. I still haven't done the exercises to correct that. I was like that with my body; I didn't quite want to correct my idiosyncrasies. I'm not an exercise person and I had a kind of jealous guarding of whatever was idiosyncratic about my movement. Though I needed to correct movement patterns sometimes, for example, to do contact and not get hurt. There were things about my posture that I didn't like and wanted to correct, I was hyper-extended and I did over a long period of time improve that, but there were other things that I didn't want to correct. Anyway, I was making very careful choices.

Jacky: Your body liked the feeling of its experience and emotional/historical information for better or worse?

Lisa: I was very stubborn. I felt like I knew what I wanted to cultivate and I was shy to say what it was, it was private. Because I wasn't achieving it necessarily, I didn't want it to be measured from the outside. I didn't want to compromise whatever little identity I felt connected to. My body was my expression, my imagination. Maybe I also had in me the memory of what it was before I started studying formal dance. At least I had had a lot of reminders that there was something special already in place, and I had experienced getting it covered up during those years of studying Graham and Ballet.

Jacky: Could you talk a little more about your relationship to choreography now, and how you craft movement.

Lisa: Even though I'm an improvisational performer, I craft movement through inner focuses. I try to narrow the movement palette down through various kinds of relationships such as the relationship between my vision and my breathing. I don't memorize movement, but I craft movement. Steve and I made one piece together called *PA RT* that had an open score for movement; it was the only performance piece where I didn't craft the movement palette in advance and was the least choreographic score of any dance I have ever made. We performed it occasionally, like once a year, for about 24 years. The piece had an underlying sound score of Robert Ashley's[13] opera '*Private Parts*' and a structure of solo, duet, solo, duet and costumes we had assembled from clothes at hand, and minimal masks – sunglasses on Steve, a small drawn moustache on me. These elements seemed to be a very strong frame for us, a vehicle for a dialogue between us, so we somehow kept doing it. Because I didn't have a movement crafting score, it was like performing 'dancing' which I've never otherwise done.

Jacky: How did the video work integrate with your dance making?

Lisa: I have always, rather reluctantly, made solos out of necessity because you just have to have them as a performer. But mostly I have worked in collaboration with other artists, usually one on one. By the 1980s I was teaching video to dancers and film-makers and composition and vocal work in workshops. All these activities were made up of the same material – the co-teaching material – creating a grab bag of feedback systems for learning, self teaching, communication and collaboration. By 1984 or so it started to get very cumbersome to teach video the way I was teaching it, because it was so much about getting equipment together while touring. I got sick of it and I realized I didn't need the video to teach what I was teaching. I had distilled feedback systems and exercises to create mirrored explorations on both sides of the camera. You were doing the same thing whether you had the camera or not.

Jacky: Both groups, as it were, were in the seeing role?

Lisa Nelson dancing with Steve Paxton in *PA RT* at X6 Dance Space, London, 1977. Photograph: Geoff White

Lisa: Always in both. So the 'tuning scores', which were part of my teaching development at that time, got clearer and clearer as I explored them purely in movement.

Jacky: So the tuning scores became part of the creative process? Could you explain more about the tuning scores.

Lisa: Well, the scores address many questions I found elemental in watching dance, and particularly western concert dance and thus western improvisational dance. The feedback forms I found offered me a way to address the question of what we see when we are looking at a dance. How do dancers think? How do we make choices? How does dance 'mean' to a dancer? There are many group or duet tuning scores which are improvisational composition or real-time editing practices. And there is a solo practice that underlies the group activity. If I can say this very briefly, they're all based on instant feedback, showing each other what we see, what we value, recycling our vision and tuning in the dance that arises in the space. The dancers use two kinds of action tools: their movement and vocal calls, like 'end', 'pause', 'reverse', 'replace', 'report', etc., to make a satisfying experience for themselves while clearly communicating their desires to the group. Each player is performer, director and spectator at the same time, so we are completely interdependent. And the practice itself is a performance in itself. The scores also slow down the process fuelling the dance, which allows for detailed discussion afterwards about each person's perception of a moment of action. It is greatly satisfying to have a process to assess the dance both as it is happening and afterwards.

In 1990, just after we finished building our studio in Vermont, some dancers came to work with me and we got involved with these scores together for the next 8 years.

Jacky: Was that Image Lab?

Lisa: That became Image Lab, which we named after several years – a core group with Karen Nelson, KJ Holmes and Scott Smith.

Jacky: So tuning is about communication, seeing, listening and fine tuning the senses?

Lisa: Right, tuning our senses and our perception of form. Playing with our opinions and making something together. Composition/choreography for me wasn't about design, it wasn't about the organization of the outside; it was about how the body organizes itself to relate to the environment inside and around you which is ever changing. So it's observation of that constant tuning activity of the organism.

Jacky: You called your workshops the observatories?

Lisa: I called public showings of the tuning practice 'Observatories', because people can come and observe themselves observing. Because the process is slowed down, and the editing tools are simple to understand, it engages the viewer in observing their own editing process and desires while watching dance while at the same time becoming informed of what kinds of decisions dancers confront in navigating their physicality and making work.

Jacky: Do you involve detailed physiological information in this practice? I find that knowledge of the internal landscape encourages the imagination that you talk about. Do you do that work, do you bring that material in?

Lisa: I don't offer great detail. I try to give enough physiological references to the genetic design of the human sense organs and the synaesthesia that feeds our ability to organize a perception and assess our body's own way of making choices. But I don't remember details myself, and in essence I don't have the time for it in the workshops. I tell people where to go for the information about how our organisms – the neurological organism, the organs, the fluids – are designed to bring us communication and dialogue within the body systems. What I offer are practices, models of exploration for observing oneself connect with the environment through movement. I'm offering interlocking but simple maps of what you might observe which can lead you to wanting further anatomical information. I try and ground the explorations in the physical as much as possible through discussion and practice. It links to the awareness I really wish to see in looking at dancers and that I don't see very much, and I feel like a beginner – I mean it's just so slow.

Jacky: That's good to hear – I feel like that too! You have described a wonderful and interesting journey and a process that I can imagine will sustain and feed you and make you inquisitive for the rest of your life. Can I ask you, therefore, how you feel about getting older? Particularly as you have said you felt like a beginner, that you will just grow and keep growing, and that you have actually found a way of working.

Lisa: I was dancing less in those first few years working with Image Lab. I was about 40 and I started to watch my physicality and my energy begin to atrophy. I was sitting on my arse for 4 months a year making two *Contact Quarterly*[14] magazines. I was farming 5 months a year and I had to travel to teach the rest of the year; any extra time I had I was researching with Image Lab who were a joy to work with. I was starting to worry that I wasn't dancing enough. Then, at 47, I got ill and I knew I had to change things, take care of my body. I had uterine fibroids and had no energy moving through the centre of my body, I couldn't even get up in one piece from the ground and stand. So I was deciding whether to stop dancing, because my options for healing were to have surgery, a quick solution with ominous future consequences, or wait years in the chance the fibroids would go away with menopause. Around this period I was on a long 7-week tour with a group of people, including performing *PA RT* with Steve, dancing more than I had in years and doing tons of teaching and being very active but struggling with energy because of the fibroids. Then, at the next to the last performance of the tour, all my dancing came back! It came back as if I was 20 years younger and I felt it was because I was finally dancing enough. It felt incredible. I was just completely taken, transported, my body re-appearing out of nowhere. I understood then that in order to keep dancing I had to find the way t dance more.

Lisa Nelson leading a workshop in Brussels 2005. Photograph: © Raymond Mallentjer

Jacky: Have you been dancing?

Lisa: I haven't quite enough, but I have been making more time for it. So when I'm travelling to teach or perform, I have been making tuning projects with small groups, either with colleagues or students, where I can dance more. I'm aware of what I have lost in my movement imagination. When I had the fibroids it was apparent to me that my imagination was still moving in the exact same way but my body wouldn't follow, as it is with any injury or time of change with the body. My ageing body carries the spectre of never reclaiming its physical imagination on the level that I was used to. So that was frustrating at first; my nervous system prepared to move but it wasn't able to follow through. Now I'm more used to it and I am growing new patterns from a new imagination. I'm not as reflexive as I used to be – provoking of accidents and surprise in my own movement – because I don't move fast for very long. But I'm finding another way that is really interesting – it delivers something else. In any case, though I find it shocking to have become a demographic – an old(er) dancer, I love looking at a mature dancer who tastes every moment of their movement.

Vermont, USA, August 2005

Notes

1. Juilliard: New York dance, drama and music school, offering pre-professional conservatory training.
2. Pearl Lang (1921–2009): US dancer, choreographer and teacher renowned as an interpreter and propagator of the choreographic style of Martha Graham, and also for her own long-time dance company, the Pearl Lang Dance Theater.
3. Bennington College: a liberal arts college located in Bennington, Vermont, USA. The college was founded in 1932 as a women's college and became co-educational in 1969.
4. Release technique: an umbrella term encompassing a variety of different body practices that emphasize efficiency of movement. Emphasis is placed on breath, skeletal alignment, joint articulation, ease of muscular tension and the use of gravity and momentum to facilitate movement.
5. Bonnie Bainbridge Cohen: developer of Body-Mind Centering® and the founder and educational director of the Body-Mind Centering School. For over 35 years she has been an innovator and leader in developing an embodied and integrated approach to movement, touch and repatterning, experiential anatomy and psychophysical processes. She is the author of the book, *Sensing, Feeling and Action*.
6. Steve Paxton: see interview p. 87 and biography p. 192.
7. Daniel Nagrin (1917–2008): US modern dancer, choreographer, teacher and author.
8. Joseph Chaikin (1935 to 2003:) an American theatre director, playwright and pedagogue. In 1963 he founded The Open Theater, a theatre co-operative that progressed from a closed experimental laboratory to a performance ensemble.

9. Judson Dance Theater: an informal group of dancers who performed at the Judson Memorial Church, New York, between 1962 and 1964. The group of artists that formed Judson Dance Theater are considered the founders of postmodern dance. The theatre grew out of a dance composition class taught by Robert Dunn, a musician who had studied with John Cage. The artists involved with Judson Dance Theater were avant-garde experimentalists who rejected the confines of modern dance practice and theory.

10. Robert Dunn (1928–96): US musician and choreographer who led classes in dance composition, contributing to the birth of the postmodern dance period in the early 1960s in New York City.

11. Nancy Stark Smith: US dancer, author, organizer and founding participant in contact improvisation. In 1975, she founded *Contact Quarterly*, an international journal of dance and improvisation, which she continues to edit with Lisa Nelson.

12. Daniel Lepkoff: US dancer who participated in the first public showing of contact improvisation in 1972 and was a central figure in its subsequent development. He is a founder of Movement Research in New York City and teaches and performs world-wide.

13. Robert Ashley: a contemporary American composer, best known for his operas and other theatrical works, many of which incorporate electronics and extended techniques.

14. Contact Quarterly (CQ): founded in 1975, CQ is a biennial journal of dance, improvisation, performance and contemporary movement arts devoted to the dancer's voice. Published in the United States it has a wide international readership.

Chapter 3

Dance is the Best Cream and the Best Vitamin

La Tati

Fergus: I'd like to know a little bit about how you learned to dance.

La Tati: I probably started dancing when I was born, because I can't remember! I was born in a barrio of Madrid where singing and dancing were just a part of life, where many Andalusian and gitanos lived. When I was seven, a teacher from Seville came to the Rastro area in Madrid and that's when I went to the studio and took my first lessons.

Fergus: Did your family come originally from Madrid, or was it from Andalucia?

La Tati: They come from all over – from Santander, in the north of Spain, from the South, different parts.

Fergus: What was it like at the studio?

La Tati: I was invited to come and take a class, but I had no money at that time and so I did the chores around the studio, the cleaning and so on, I took care of the studio. I slept in the studio, putting six chairs together. I learned from just watching and listening. When I was 11, my teacher broke her ankle, and that's when I offered to teach her classes! I had learned everything in the repertory of the school – flamenco, classical, castanets, everything. I made my professional debut at 12.

Fergus: And you danced professionally from then?

La Tati: Yes, yes. And later my career divided and I became a choreographer and teacher as well. I give courses and lectures on the theory and history of flamenco, and since 1986 I've had my own company.

Jacky: It seems to us that, unlike ballet or modern dancers, flamenco dancers are more respected as they become more mature. Is this true?

La Tati: In flamenco, age *is* important. If you've had a fruitful working career, your experience counts for a lot. Your physical abilities are not as important, because it's not how high you lift your leg, it's *how* you lift it. It's like theatre. Flamenco has a lot in common with theatre. You're dealing with time. You grow up with time. Of course you need to be physically healthy.

Jacky: You gain wisdom in your body?

La Tati: Very much so. You have to work with a strong consciousness of what you are doing.

Fergus: Yes, and you can be more conscious the more you know.

La Tati dancing in the 1990s. Photograph: René Robert

La Tati: Yes, your memories and your different experiences all contribute.

Fergus: This is something we appreciated very much in your performance. I had the impression that you could play with the technique – you didn't just have to do it, you could play with it.

La Tati: Yes, even though I am performing so seriously, I enjoy it so much. I heard an artist say once that he wanted to die on stage … I take the opposite view, I *live* for the stage, I don't want to die on stage, I live for it! Dance is the best cream and the best vitamin!

Fergus: As a dancer, do you feel very different now to when you were 20?

La Tati: Yes. Of course. My love for the arts has always been something intuitive, but now I know how to put things into perspective, into place. Undoubtedly I dance differently now. Now I savour each moment. Nowadays I've lost all ambition to be rich and famous. So now that I don't expect anything I feel so free! When you're 20 that's your goal, to become rich and famous. I'm not so breathless now; it's much more gratifying, it's much more beautiful – it becomes a very spiritual feeling.

Jacky: I also very much saw you as the actor-dancer: within your dancing there were some fantastic characters being explored …

La Tati: Yes. There's a transformation from the tablao, the small café where flamenco comes from, into the theatre. Since 1994, I've been doing a form of flamenco theatre, using actors and speech. That's my project for the future. That's what I want to do – I don't know if it will be possible, but that's what I want to do.

Fergus: But also flamenco has such a drama within the pure dance.

La Tati: Flamenco artists are really very theatrical and dramatic, but most people don't capitalize on that, they don't realize it. It comes from the suffering of the race and the culture.

Jacky: I also loved the humour and the playfulness. It was very funny as well.

La Tati: It all depends on which dance I'm interpreting. For example, the dance from Cadiz is very open to the ocean, the Atlantic, the salt. Other dances are much more sad and have another tempo. It's a corporal expression. You express with your face and body everything you feel.

Jacky: How do you train, how do you keep fit?

La Tati: I don't usually keep to a training schedule. When I'm not performing I go to the theatre, I read, I see other groups. I teach my dance classes. When I have to prepare for a production like this one, then I go into the studio and train myself.

Fergus: And when you are preparing for a production, is the training just doing the dances themselves, or is there another training as well?

La Tati: I visualize the structure of the piece and when I have a structure I start making decisions about the music and how to present it for an audience. Then it becomes physical.

Fergus: I understand. But I had an even more basic question, which is, is there an exercise regime, or not?

Jacky: It's interesting, everyone we have spoken to has a very special and unique preparation process. Everyone adapts and finds their own personal way.

La Tati: Yes. I meditate and I stretch. And I walk, walk, walk. But the dances, that's really the work, because I anyway teach about 3 hours of classes and I work through those as well. My classes are intermediate and advanced, so they are demanding. They are both choreography and technique, so I do a lot of work.

Teaching and studying now have changed. It's become impersonal now. There's no longer a relationship between the teacher and the pupil. I think the teacher has an obligation to teach more than just steps or it becomes something orthopaedic.

Jacky: To bring it back to the theme of age, in western classical and modern dance companies, dancers are traditionally considered old at 35! It's part of the oppression.

La Tati: Yes. It is oppressive, but I've seen very great artists over 40. Young dancers today are in a hurry to push out the older dancers. They are in a hurry to get there, so they have to step on other people! The myth has arisen that you have to be very young with a beautiful shape to be an artist. But the art is in the artist and in the transmission, not in the physical shape. There could be a beautiful woman beside you, but if you are an artist, you are that much more beautiful. The audience vibrates with what they see. As long as they pay for the tickets …!

Fergus: Do women in flamenco tend to dance longer than men?

La Tati: Historically, yes. The women go on longer.

Fergus: Why?

La Tati: I don't know! [Laughs] Because women are better than men!

Fergus: Yes. Stronger …

La Tati: Stronger. And also we have a sense of sacrifice. Whether it's in the genes, hormonal, in our education or the way our parents raised us – we must go on and on and on. We have much more of an internal struggle that keeps us going longer. And we have necessities that are not known, not visible. The well-known figures nowadays are all men – Joachin Cortes,[1] you know. There are women in Spain who have great capacity, not only as dancers but also as choreographers – like myself, but the leading artists are men. The women have always struggled to find a position in the art form. In gypsy culture the men are very jealous and protective of the women. The women are not supposed to have brains, they are just supposed to dance.

Fergus: Is there not a tradition of people like Carmen Amaya,[2] or was she exceptional?

La Tati: There was a time when there were great women figures – Pilar Lopez,[3] Rosario,[4] but those women were of another era, and Carmen Amaya was unusual because she toured with her whole family, all her uncles and cousins … the others were also different because they were involved in classical Spanish dance, that was a different training and tradition altogether. But in flamenco the women have always been on the side. It's a very male macho world and now that we're liberated … here come the men and take our position anyway!

Jacky: So practitioners like you are really challenging the status quo?

La Tati: In my case, I support my whole family. I'm the mother and father of the family, so I really run everything. No one's ever given me anything for free.

Jacky: You're also a choreographer. How important to you is it to both choreograph and perform?

Fergus: Because we've noticed that with all the people we've talked to, who have carried on, who are still working, they are all also creative artists, they are choreographers, as well as performers.

La Tati: Choreographing has given me a wider range of expression. A choreographer also has to transmit feeling. There you are leaving part of your soul. If you're going to explain something it has to be very clear, it has to be transparent. One day, when I retire, I would like to continue as a choreographer. I like to choreograph, but I also like to be able to act, to interpret. When I am choreographing, I am totally dedicated to the choreography. If I'm walking down the street, whatever I'm doing, I'm thinking about my choreography. I could be eating and I would leave my food to finish off a step. It absorbs everything.

When you dance, you show everything that you know. Like the earth, you water it and it gives up fruit.

Fergus: And would you say that flamenco is in the process of a change at the moment?

La Tati: It's been changing over the last 20 years. The process is slow. There is a change. Flamenco has a trunk. You can't go too far with it. The tree will maybe give different coloured leaves every once in a while, but it's still the same tree. It's still the same traditional culture. Within that culture the evolution of flamenco takes place. Flamenco is a very emotional, individualistic and intimate form. Each person will interpret it their way, but they must always remember where the roots are. Otherwise it evaporates, it loses its force, its freshness. You can't learn it in a book or in a university, it's something you have to live and experience.

Jacky: Do you have to start as a child?

La Tati: Yes, it's convenient, though it's not always like that. Some people have started at the age of 20, but today when it is becoming much more technical, it's useful to start early

Fergus: Is it too late for me?

La Tati: [Laughs] It doesn't matter! It's a way of life!

Jacky: The structure of the show that you are performing is wonderful, because it's structured so that each person has their solo and when the company comes together, it's this extraordinary ensemble – each person is a star. It's fantastic.

La Tati: I'm happy you see it that way. Some people don't understand that – we have comments like: 'What's that young boy doing, is that flamenco or is he just mimicking?' Flamenco is any age. It doesn't matter.

La Tati dancing as a young girl. Photograph permission of La Tati

Jacky: And with the young boy, the core was there.

La Tati: It's normal that a young person should imitate older dancers, but in flamenco you have your own personality: these boys are already formed at this age. They are already in a career. They are not imitating, they are being who they are. That's what we wanted to do - present generations of flamenco.

Fergus: You were talking about intimacy in performance, and what's wonderful is that you manage to generate intimacy in a big theatre.

La Tati: Yes it's important to transmit that passion – it's very warm and hot. So no matter how small a gesture is, it just comes right out.

Jacky: Do you still feel there are things to learn?

La Tati: Oh, still plenty to learn. Every day!

London, UK, 10 September 2010

Notes

1. Joachin Cortés: Spanish dancer, well known for his fusion of flamenco, ballet and modern dance.
2. Carmen Amaya (1913–63): considered by many to be the greatest flamenco dancer of her time, she revolutionized flamenco by performing zapateado – the fast and complex rhythmic footwork previously only danced by men.
3. Pilar Lopez (1912–2008): Spanish dancer, teacher and choreographer, she sought to fuse classical and flamenco traditions of music and dance.
4. Rosario: Rosario Montoya Manzano, known as La Farruca and a member of the famous Farucco flamenco dynasty.

Chapter 4

Can't ... Try ... Can

Julyen Hamilton

Julyen Hamilton in his piece *How it is Made*, Berlin, 2008. Photograph: Jenny Haack

Jacky: What made you start dancing?

Julyen: It was the solution to the problem of what to do with life; more specifically it was a solution to how my incredible enjoyment of physical work could be integrated. I was a gymnast; I loved gymnastics and had done many competitions, so in that sense I was a performer. We took trampolining to country fetes and in a way we taught each other how the body moves within these forms. Being in the backwaters of Suffolk, we didn't really have a teacher, and so we had to make up lots of things and when we got a move we shared it with our sparring partners whom sometimes we beat or who sometimes beat us in all the competitions because no one else was around.

So all that physicality saved me psychologically in childhood and adolescence.

And a whole other stream, which normally through schooling was kept worlds apart, was a love of poetry, a love of theatre. I did big parts at school, learning massive texts; I loved to be on stage, loved to be speaking or talking – I loved declamation. I adored the action; it wasn't a question of the competition, I just loved reciting a poem, or reading in church or anything. Suddenly I discovered dance and it was 'AAH, they go together – I can be physical and I can be on stage and perform' … it clicked, it was totally clear and made sense. What had been two different poles came together in this art form.

Fergus: Where did you find it?

Julyen: I was in Cambridge retaking A levels to try and get into University, which I knew I didn't want to do. I wanted to get my teeth into something because I knew that was how I learnt. In Cambridge I got involved with acting and in one of the projects Liebe Klug[1] was doing the movement for *The Tempest* and I was one of the two Ariels who were dressed hermaphroditically, bisexual or asexual. All these things made a lot of sense to me; the female sensibility that was in all the poetry and literature which I felt at home with and another sort of viscerality which was portrayed much more as a male side – this character who didn't speak much but moved a lot in a speaking context. When Liebe said 'You have to move like that before you say those lines' I just knew how to put it together – and so she invited me to join her company.

During that time a group called Strider[2] (you were in the company Jacky) came to Cambridge to perform. We did the opening part of the programme, they did the second part and I stood up in the middle of it and said 'I want to do that' before realizing with embarrassment that I was in the audience. Afterwards I just went and asked you all how do you do it – I said 'I want to be a dancer'; and from then became very clear. I went to The Place [London Contemporary Dance School] and spoke to Pat Hutchinson[3] and asked if I could get in. She said they would give it a thought; I said I was going back on the train and could she tell me now please – and luckily, dear eccentric that she was, she saw that it was heartfelt and said yes – I don't know what rules she was breaking!

Fergus: What is your attitude to your body now, and how is it different from what it was back then?

Julyen: In my family there were never any specific body taboos; we were naked at home, we saw each other naked. There was respect when we were adolescent for both myself and my sister, but I never gained from my mother or my father any fear of body, or prudery of body. My mother is disabled; it is not an issue. Due to her courage and hard work and my father's silent support it gave me an ease with my body. But in my body there was a bundle of rage, a bundle of frustration with my schooling – I wanted a more creative schooling and saw through all the rules and saw that that system wasn't working. I was furious with that and that fury was coming out when I was doing physical work – but so much had to come out and nearly all of my time at The Place I was in sequential injury because my psychology was clearing through. So the training was my saviour, but it was also nearly ruinous and I sustained a number of injuries. Now I have got through them and I don't suffer from them – they gave me hell – I was constantly tearing my muscles as I was working in a very muscular way. But I see it now I had to go through that. Beneath that there was a respect for the body – that's why I mentioned my parents – in a very simple physiological sense. So that I had a deep ground to go back to.

At that point I remember wanting to have a body that could continue to move for a long time. There was a bit of me that said : No, my body can continue – very naïvely because at that time there were very few, if any, role models for continuing after 30 or 35.

Jacky: But you were very aware of the mind body connection and your psychology working through your body?

Julyen: I can say that more clearly now than I could then. But I was aware of something going on, I was aware with my passion rather than my intellect. The confusion was real, but the passion underneath was also real. I think 19- or 20-year olds have an amazing sort of wisdom; it is a beautiful thing, it is not a tested wisdom, it is raw material, untempered.

I think also that I was interested in theatre – in Peter Brook[4], in Laurence Olivier[5] – I remember seeing Ralph Richardson[6] turn up to a Camden school to talk to us kids. We were doing the National Youth Theatre and he was 80, yet he got back on his motor bike and went phut phut back through London. And I thought, well, he's still an artist; I saw him in *Home* with Gielgud when they were both over 75. I wanted this for my art form. My model was theatre and I'd seen it work well on two levels: firstly the spread of ages all working together and secondly working in a multi-national way. The first day in Liebe's company there was a Trinidadian male nurse, a housewife, a female alternative bookshop owner, an Indonesian student and myself, and I said to myself 'Home …!'

Jacky: Are you still interested in the relationship between dance and theatre?

Julyen: For me the base is moving. I'm a dancer, if you want to put a name to it. Not because that's the supreme thing, but because somewhere I feel that's the most intelligent thing for me, or at least when I'm dancing I feel most intelligent. I feel I'm more connected to outside and inside when I'm moving. I think better when I move. It's a bit like the comedy writers who work in pairs and one is a sitter and writer and the other one is a pacer up and down – I'm a pacer up and down. That's why I love to teach, because you can move across the room and you know that if you can't get the thought here, you can move six paces across the room and understand what you want to say. In that way the base and key of it is always still dancing. But of course I love the spoken word, I love film, I like the different media very much. I remember at The Place receiving some feedback that I could never be a dancer because I thought too much! Now I'm clear that the trouble with dancers is that they don't think enough. This became very clear to me when studying Ki Aikido which really works on unifying the mind and the body. I love the intellect, I love thoughts and I love the body. I don't think there's a conflict there. I want both! And I know I'm not alone or eccentric in that. I don't like the thought that the body can be dislocated from the intellect or from words or whatever.

Jacky: Also, with the improvised context, the audience is witnessing and participating in your choices and they're watching the intelligence of the performers very directly. But to go back to the notion of this span of years from then till now, what are the forms that you have engaged in that have supported you as a practitioner?

Julyen: I think that T'ai Chi, although I didn't study it very deeply, let a lot of things fall into place that I had got from different lessons at The Place. I put it like that because there are certain things that are useful *because* they're difficult and actually don't work, then there are other things that help them fall into place, like a sort of catalyst. For instance, of all the Graham exercises there was not one that I left understanding or wanting ever to use again, for myself or other people, but maybe the experience of their difficulty was valuable in an attritional way. I've seen people train without a certain amount of attrition, and they miss something. For me it was said very clearly by my Ki Aikido teacher; he said 'Today we practise soft. Next day we practise hard. Both, to make metal strong. Soften in fire, then hit it with the hammer.' I think there was a passion and a harshness in the Graham technique that I gained from, suffered from, which then was released in the T'ai Chi and the Release work, which I rejected to begin with.

I must say that one thing that nourished me extraordinarily was Jon Keliehor's[7] rhythm classes. They gave me a system, and I can penetrate any music with that. He gave me fearlessness towards music. It really appealed to me. It was numeric, it was mathematical and you could get into where your heart was moving. And then in terms of nurturing, a certain amount of contact and release work, even though I actually studied it very little. But I'm lucky in that I learn very quickly. I did three or four classes with Mary Fulkerson,[8] studying her release work at Dartington Festivals and absorbed it. I worked only 6 weeks with Richard Alston,[9] but I worked on what he gave me for over 10 years. I only studied Aikido for about 6 months in all, but it totally changed me. In a way I'm working on it the whole time. I'm lucky like that, that if something makes sense, my body absorbs it, my body learns. So these little injections have been radical.

Jacky: And you seem to have made some good decisions along the way.

Julyen: Well luckily I made such a radical shift to begin with, from what I was projected towards, that making certain decisions wasn't so difficult after that, because the first shift was so extreme … but for instance, leaving the London Contemporary Dance Company after 2 weeks was hell! Cohan[10] wanted me to join and I said, No, I'm working with Rosemary Butcher.[11]

And I also wasn't really X6,[12] although I really looked up to that and was there in brotherhood, if not in actual presence – it wasn't quite my generation, I wasn't old enough, it wasn't the solution to anything for me, it was a possibility. For you guys it was the solution to something. I could see that difference and I was green by comparison.

Jacky: We'd already been through a huge journey with the ballet and the rejection of that world.

Julyen: Absolutely. And I hadn't got those co-ordinates to make a third point from. So the Contemporary Dance Theatre was offered and I said No and Cohan said, Please, we need another guy. So I did join and after 2 weeks I said I'm sorry, I can't handle it. It was very hard for me, because in those days you didn't turn that sort of job down – you'd been training for 4 years! I was working for £25 for Rosemary for a couple of concerts … You could say I was naïve, but I believed in her work, there was something true there. So after 2 weeks I had a back spasm, lifting another dancer, and I said Please will someone teach me how to lift him, because I think I might hurt myself, and they said Ah, you'll learn after a few injuries …! But to give him his due, it was Cohan who came and massaged me during performance to keep me going. I didn't know how to make up and he showed me. He was very sweet and kind to me; he was never aggressive, never pressurizing, and I didn't make it easy for him.

Jacky: And do you feel good about that decision now?

Julyen: Absolutely. It had to be. We went to Peterborough on the second week and one of the dancers said 'Ah, back in Peterborough again', and I thought no, I don't want to work for 10 years doing the same thing. Also there was another work to be done. Cohan came with Robin Howard[13] to see the earliest performance of Rosemary's at the Serpentine Gallery, and he said, 'I respect that you like this, but it's already been done in New York and we're now going further than that'. And I said, 'Bob, that's great for you. I wasn't there. I didn't go through it. I need to go through our one, now'. And he respected me for that.

Julyen Hamilton dancing on the roof of the London School of Contemporary Dance, 1976. Photograph: Chris Harris

That was where you people at X6 gave me extraordinary support, just by your existence. Just knowing that you were not adding two and two and getting an automatic four, but you were questioning, and doing something. And that made sense to me. And what's nice now is that it's as if a baton was being passed from those before us and those continuing after. I realize that some of the things I'm researching now, I'll never see the fruition of, but maybe some of the people trained by people I've trained will. I know I'm reaping from what Steve [Paxton] did, I know it, and I've told him so. You just feel that lineage being passed on. Things it's taken 15 years to work out, people can come to a workshop at 24 and they've got it immediately. It's wonderful how that genetic dispensing of material and research goes on.

Fergus: So how do you train? How do you keep fit? What's your regime?

Julyen: My regime is seasonal. I don't have a set regime. I really notice that in different seasons and different times of the year my body needs different things. So at times I will do more of a muscular kind of work and at other times I don't go anywhere near a studio for at least a week or two weeks and never warm up for a performance. At other times I want to do a three hour warm up. And breathing methods, basic Ki Aikido work, pliés, speaking, reading or writing as preparation for performance – a whole number of tools can be brought in and used where relevant. So that can range from a pumping of the body's muscular system to an absolute physiological disinvolvement with the whole thing, and sitting in a café until the very last minute. So you just monitor which one of those things is needed, and just hope you're right!

Jacky: That creative preparedness, that listening to your creative and physical needs – will your calves and your knees and your back be sufficiently engaged if you haven't actually done physical stuff?

Julyen: You see I think we are living a physical and mental existence 24 hours a day, and the only way it goes wrong is if we are disconnected, or if the mind reduces the way it is thinking of the body. It's the old story of the woman who could hardly lift a book, she was so frail, but when fire swept through her house, she moved all the furniture out. We apply ourselves when needed, and you can't fake or mess around with that. If you fully apply yourself to the simplicity of tying your shoelaces, then you're warmed up. You can do a thousand exercises – muscularize, release, imagine lots of different things – and it can have no effect on you. Practice is not the point, it's *how* you practise and whether the practice is linked to your real life at that moment. But it has to take action. When you said just listening to the body, that's true, but then if it answers that you have to do something, then you've got to go and do it! That's why I say it's pragmatic. It has to be actualized, otherwise it becomes an intellectually interesting observation.

Fergus: I understand that. But it strikes me there's another way of looking at the practice of some kind of physical training; for example, I personally have things I do regularly, but I try to look out for the days when I don't need to do them. If I'm not sure, I tend to do them and through the doing of certain things find out where I am. For example, the other day when I stepped up and down the steps for a long time, it had the function not just of warming me up but of stopping the rest of the white noise that's going on. So I find it useful to have certain things that are my routine.

Jacky: What we've discovered during this project in talking to a lot of people, is that this specific question – how do you warm up, how do you keep fit – has many more diverse and personal answers as people get older.

Julyen: There's another very practical issue. If you work with musicians, they come into the space and they're ready to start right away. They unpack their instruments and say, Let's blow! I remember a musician saying, Why do you dancers spend so much time warming up and then you're too tired to blow? So I said, OK. And five minutes before the show I warmed up. No problem.

Jacky: I made some work last year based on the ballet *Petrouchka* and I found I had to engage in the classical technique. Do you think it partly depends on the vocabulary that you want to use?

Julyen: Ironically, I find the opposite. Having not been on a trampoline for 15 years, I can do moves that I couldn't do originally, and I've found that since I stopped stretching in second, à la Graham, I was looser … I'm not very good at practising, that's the problem! I get worse and worse at practising and more and more bored with it. Thank goodness for Rubinstein[14] who said that after 40 you really shouldn't do more than 2 hours a day on the piano. But I will say that this is all because the techniques are serving *my* voice – I'm doing *my* work at *my* pace in *my* way. If I wanted to repeat steps or I wanted to be at a certain pitch in a certain way, then of course I would have to rehearse that. And you do lose techniques. I used to have this amazing ability to copy other people's steps and I was trying the other day and it was rusty, I hadn't practised it.

Jacky: To come back to a very basic question. How do you keep fit?

Julyen: Well, I have a family and I live in the country. You're walking up and down stairs, you're lifting a child, you're cutting the lawn, you're ironing, you're chopping wood, you're … I eat everything I want. I got bored with trying diets, so if I want it, I eat it. If I want to drink it, I drink it. I got so bored with restricting myself, I said, OK, have exactly what you want, when you want, and screw it – and it just solved itself. So sometimes I have a lot of alcohol and sometimes no alcohol. It's not a problem.

Jacky: So it's all part of life.

Julyen: Completely. Because I'm very bad at false disciplines. Something in me balks, and then my body goes into very bad disorder.

Fergus: Are there any non-dance things you like doing, like walking or running or swimming?

Julyen: I love walking, I love swimming, I love doing woodwork, I love mixing cement, I love moving rocks and I love building things. I love doing the cleaning, sweeping up – they're all gloves and boots stuff on a cold, fresh morning. If you took those things away from me, I would be very unhappy. Many of these activities are physical, and they do keep me fit. Fit means appropriate, so appropriate for what? If you don't have the what, fit can't plug in anywhere. But I would say that having been trained with techniques, the concept of: Can't … Try a technique … Can – those three stages of learning – is very important. I think there's a big crisis in teaching because there is often not the proposed vocabulary of difficulty and a system through which a student can pass. It's those three stages – Can't … Try … Can – which build confidence.

I read an interview with Ravi Shankar[15] recently, and two things he said moved me very deeply. One was: it's wonderful to be a great performer, but in our tradition, to be a teacher is even more revered, because you come to the end of your life as a performer, but teaching carries on the lineage. The second thing was about talent. He said: Talent is something your teacher gives you. You're not born with it. Talent, as in the biblical talent – money – is given to you by your teacher. That's what happened to me at The Place. Certain of my teachers – Jon [Keliehor], you [Fergus], Flora [Cushman],[16] gave me talent. You gave me, by the way you looked, or what was said, or not said, talent. Not just a romantic belief in 'maybe you'll make it', but talent – saying in effect – 'Now you work on that'. And in Flora's way that was a bit crazy; in Jon's way it was very mathematical; and from you, Fergus, it was silent. I respected that. It was silent but with a challenge, with a sternness. I was frightened of you – but I wasn't frightened of you as a person, I was frightened because it was as if you were saying 'Here is something, now you get on with that, you make sure you get on with that.' So then reading very recently this thing from Ravi Shankar, all these things fell into place.

Jacky: What has been your most enjoyable performing experience to date?

Julyen: One of the most satisfying series of performances I've done has been the Forty Monologues project. The idea was to do 40 pieces – 20-minute monologues – and they would be poetic improvisations that weren't just like open blows, but each one had to have a poetic integrity to it. I did three in an evening, and I would number them sequentially. After 39, I decided that this thing was still rolling, so now I'm up to about 65 and it's continuing. That has been very satisfying for me; it's accruing, accumulating something. Because when you improvise, you just make so many performances and that's it, they're gone. Sometimes it tears on the heart, because you get very attached to things that are made.

Now I'm trying to branch out from the experience of the monologues into a group situation – what can you do with five that you can't do with one? And I've also been making pieces for fifteen and twenty people. So I've posed the question: what is an instant composition made by a number of people at the same time? How can four or five people be instantly creative together, in performance? I'm therefore directing. I call that directing, because I don't think choreography is the right word.

Jacky: And are you feeling pleased with the group work?

Julyen: Yes. It's great. You do with five what you can't do with one. Those different numbers are wonderful. I'm also liking larger groups. This is a social and communal thing. I've been showing work with twenty people all improvising at the same time. It's very interesting that you don't usually see that. We think in terms of one or two people, a small family group, or a football crowd! We don't often eat as a group of fifteen, therefore we're not

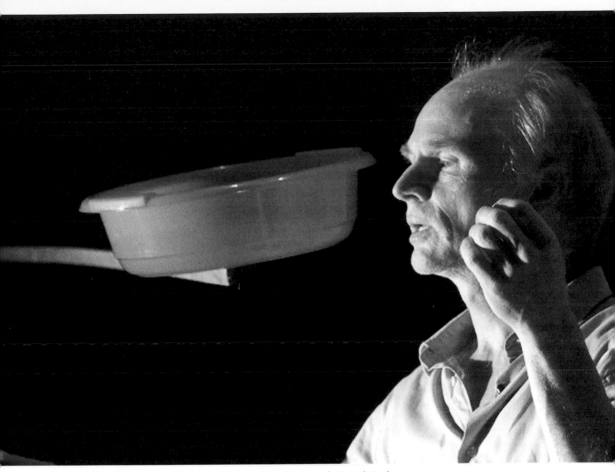

Julyen Hamilton in *How It Is Made*, Belgium 2010. Photograph: Patrick Beelaert

used to seeing fifteen minds and bodies alive and alert together, and I think it's a very beautiful thing. It's a very lovely communal area which we can share. It's also for me a political statement, to see people creative together. It's not committee work, it's a deep communal intertrust and responsibility. Because I think we are incredibly creative. It's always the unknown quantifier in all historical calculations of how the future's going to be – they just don't put into the equation human creativity, and it's so abundant that it's messing up all predictions for the future.

London 30 May 1998

Notes

1. Liebe Klug: Cambridge-based choreographer and teacher.
2. Strider (1972–75): often described as Britain's first postmodern dance company, was formed by Richard Alston, Jacky Lansley, Di Davies, Dennis Greenwood, Wendy Levett, Christopher Banner and Sally Potter.
3. Patricia Hutchinson Mackenzie: Principal, London Contemporary Dance School 1968–76.
4. Peter Brook CH, CBE: an influential English theatre and film director and innovator, who has been based in France since the early 1970s. He was the director of the experimental Bouffes du Nord in Paris for 36 years.
5. Laurence Olivier, OM (1907–89): an English actor, director, and producer. He was the first director of the National Theatre and was one of the most famous and revered actors of the 20th century.
6. Sir Ralph Richardson (1902–83): was an English actor, one of a group of theatrical knights of the mid-20th century who, though more closely associated with the stage, also appeared in several classic films.
7. Jon Keliehor: Scottish-based composer and percussionist, he taught percussion at the London School of Contemporary Dance in the 1970s; his music is widely used by dancers and performance artists in the United Kingdom, the United States and Venezuela.
8. Mary O'Donnell Fulkerson: US dancer, choreographer and teacher of release-based work, she is a Fellow of Dartington College, United Kingdom and directed dance schools in Germany and the Netherlands before returning to the United States. She is the author of a book: *Release, Seven Zones of Comprehension Coming from the Practice of Dance*.
9. Richard Alston: UK choreographer, founder of Strider and formerly director of the Rambert Dance Company, now artistic director of The Place and of the Richard Alston Dance Company.
10. Robert Cohan: US dancer and choreographer, originally soloist with Martha Graham and later founding director of the London Contemporary Dance Theatre.
11. Rosemary Butcher: UK independent choreographer and teacher; has been making innovative works for more than 3 decades. She is based in London and is a Senior Researcher at the University of Middlesex.
12. X6 Dance Space: experimental dance studio and performance space 1976–80, run by a collective including Emilyn Claid, Maedée Duprès, Fergus Early, Jacky Lansley and Mary Prestidge.

13. Robin Howard (1924–83): founder of the Contemporary Dance Trust which encompasses the London Contemporary Dance School, London Contemporary Dance Theatre (now Richard Alston Dance Company) and The Place Theatre.
14. Arthur Rubinstein (1887–1982): Polish-American pianist, regarded as one of the finest pianists of the 20th century.
15. Ravi Shankar: renowned Indian classical sitar player who did much to popularize Indian music in the West and to explore fusions of Indian and western classical musics.
16. Flora Cushman: teacher and choreographer at the London Contemporary Dance School in the early 1970s, now teaching and choreographing in Israel.

Chapter 5

There are So Many Surprises

Yoshito Ohno

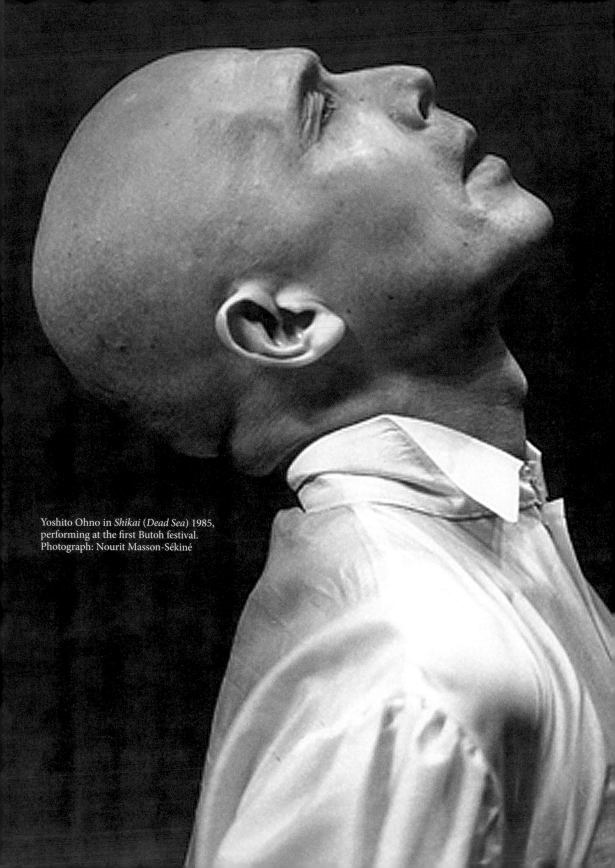

Yoshito Ohno in *Shikai* (*Dead Sea*) 1985,
performing at the first Butoh festival.
Photograph: Nourit Masson-Sékiné

We arrived very early at Yoshito's studio in a leafy suburb of Yokahama – its sign was almost concealed; it was raining. We caught a glimpse of Yoshito in the house kitchen next door – preparing dinner; there was a huge pile of vegetables on the table. He gestured to us to enter the studio, we did, removing shoes first, and it felt a little damp. The studio, built in the 60s to accommodate the work of his father, Kazuo Ohno,[1] has a theatrical feel to it; old hats, scarves, shoes, fans are stacked in a corner and built in cupboards full of costumes accumulated over decades are along the whole of one wall. There are shelves of mementoes – dolls, statues, plastic flowers, glittery things; and of course there is the low table and mats for tea.

Yoshito arrived bringing tea and little traditional snacks. He is a warm and charming person with bright lively eyes that always look directly at you; he tilts his head coquettishly, determinedly light. We began the interview explaining our themes and questions. Practically immediately he was up physically demonstrating the ideas he wanted to share – sometimes he would draw pictures and diagrams or write words to support what he was trying to express. Our translator Yoko Nishimura did well – he seemed to trust her and enjoy the opportunity that a good translator presented; he dropped in the occasional and perfectly apt English word.

Fergus: When did you start to dance?

Yoshito: I started dance, when I was 13 years old, when I was in high school. My father told me to come to his studio, but I wanted to play football so I told him I didn't want to go.

It was just after the war so for men to be dancing was rare and it felt embarrassing to be dancing, but my mother said 'Yoshito, please go' and I couldn't say no to my mum.

Kazuo Ohno was teaching in a girl's high school at the time, a mission school, so I would have to dance with all women students at the studio. And that felt embarrassing.

My mother said, 'Your dad has been inventing and thinking and trying out new dance and he would like to teach you so please go and learn from him.'

So, my father was drumming and saying 'ichi ni san, ni ni san (*one, two, three: Yoshito demonstrates a waltzing movement*) … ichi ni san, ni ni san, san ni san, shi ni san' - he started dance lessons like this; and he always taught us how to walk – like this (*Yoshito demonstrates the walking exercise*) 'Don't do it like that … do it like this … lift your chest up, pull your chin in … In daily life your posture is like this and like that … but in the studio, we need to pull in the chin, like this … and it is very difficult.'

This was the training I did 'ichi ni san, ni ni san, san ni san, shi ni san' and then there was the free dancing time.

FREE!! Kaaaaaa! … (*Yoshito improvises freely*)

Jacky: You were improvising?

Yoshito: Yes, half of the time was free style, half of the time was training. What was most difficult was that he would say, 'the flower is beautiful.' I was puzzled. He kept saying 'the flower is beautiful, the flower is beautiful.' But I thought, 'you say the flower is beautiful but how can I do art when everyday life is difficult because of poverty and everyone is suffering; what is he talking about – the flower is beautiful!' (*Everyone laughs*). There was great poverty, it was very hard.

Jacky: After the war?

Yoshito: Yes. In a situation like that where people were suffering and you get told 'the flower is beautiful,' I felt khaaaaaaa. So in the studio I said 'the flower is not beautiful' I was always thinking that in the studio.

Fergus: So when did you first start to perform?

(*Yoshito goes to the cupboard and brings out a poster*)

Yoshito: My first performance was *Black Dance*. Tatsumi Hijikata[2] called it *Ankoku Buyo* (*Dance of Utter Darkness*).[3] I danced this in 1959 when I was 20 years old with Tatsumi Hijikata, it was a duet. It was called *Kinjiki*[4] (*Forbidden Colour*). That was my first performance. I didn't know what the theme was but I asked 'what is it – because the two of us dance like this?' (*Yoshito demonstrates standing and putting his arms and hands in an upward gesture*) and I was told it is about men's true friendship. So of course one of the elements it was exploring was homosexuality. It was the first homosexual dance which had been performed and the audience was shocked. For 7 years from that time, I danced many pieces together with Tatsumi Hijikata and also with Kazuo Ohno.

Fergus: And did Hijikata Tatsumi choreograph the work?

Yoshito: Yes he did.

Jacky: So the pieces were all very structured. Were there any improvised sections?

Yoshito: For my part, it was all choreographed, but for Kazuo Ohno, it was all improvisation. Always improvisation.

In Japanese you write 'person' like this (*writing 人 on paper*), it's a kanji character.

So, this long line could be Tatsumi Hijikata and this short line supporting could be Kazuo Ohno; or maybe it is the other way round and this long line could be Kazuo Ohno and this short line supporting could be Tatsumi Hijikata. It could be either. They were two totally different people in opposite and different places collaborating and making something as one.

For example, there were the famous writers Yukio Mishima[5] and Tatsuhiko Shibusawa[6] – two well-known authors from the same university and very close as well, but the way they thought was completely different and they had completely different interests. Yukio Mishima saw the performance *Kinjiki* and then brought Tatsuhiko Shibusawa to see it. They then brought all sorts of other people to the show such as poets, painters, fashion designers, musicians, composers; people like Takemitsu[7] who would become well known later on; all these people started to gather around the work. But it was Yukio Mishima who initially saw the show and began this interest. Both these authors had a different view on what the beauty was – Kazuo Ohno and Tatsumi Hijikata were both so different – which allowed the audience to view and approach the work from different directions.

If you just look at Mishima san and Shibusawa san's books, I think you'll see their difference. He (Tatsuhiko Shibusawa) puts the importance on the form; on the other hand, Mishima is not satisfied only with the form, it needs to also have the scent of death.

When he (Yukio Mishima) was 45, he committed suicide by Harakiri.

Jacky: So – this is maybe over simplistic – the work is about bringing opposites together; or opposites working side by side? It was extraordinary that Tatsumi Hijikata and Kazuo Ohno should meet.

Yoshito: A miracle meeting! (*Yoshito's hands are constantly expressive and repeatedly come together in an almost prayer like position suggesting a meeting*). Tatsumi Hijikata brought the darkness into the dance, and Kazuo Ohno brought the light – this meeting brought about the world of Butoh.

Jacky: Ankoku Butoh means dance of darkness. Does your work still concern itself with darkness? You mentioned that you are working on a dance about holocaust which concerns Hiroshima, Auschwitz and Pompeii. Do you think it is important for artists to explore these issues and events?

Yoshito: Yes. I have always been wondering 'what is darkness?' Watching Hijikata san dance, I always wondered what darkness is … (*Yoshito goes to the table and draws a diagram of dates and locations*). He was born in Akita prefecture, North of Japan in 1928. I was born '38, Kazuo Ohno '06. At the time in 1929, the world banks, like now, went boom! The depression happened. So Tatsumi Hijikata was in the north, in Akita, and he was like this … cold … cold and always hungry (*Yoshito stands and moves into a shivering, crouching position. His shoulders are hunched forward and his arms hanging down in front; his hands are stiff with straight fingers. Throughout the interview Yoshito's hands are constantly moving and often very directional*). So his body was like this … and like this … that came out in his dance; that's the darkness – and that's his daily life.

Hosoe Eiko[8] made two photography books on Tatsumi Hijikata. This is Hosoe san's *The Body of Light and Darkness* (*Yoshito shows us the book – reference is made to Hijikata's Dance of Experience performance events in which the audience's experience was central*).

Jacky: The performers look so contemporary. It is as though the past, present and future have all collapsed into each other.

Yoshito: Exactly. Human nature doesn't change.
I often think about changing things and unchanging things.
The civilization changes but not human nature.
That's important.

Jacky: That the human nature stays intact?

Yoshito: Yes the human nature not changing is important.

Jacky: We saw that you had a big gap in performing; you stopped performing and had a comeback in 1985. Why was that?

Yoshito: Yes that's right, I was 46 or 45 when I decided to come back; he, Tatsumi Hijikata, was worried.

Fergus: Worried? Why?

Yoshito: I was away from performing for 17 years. I didn't actually hear directly from him but someone told me that he was worried. We had worked together from when I was 20 until I was 27 years old; everyone remembers me as brilliant. So after all these years, being older, if the performance was not great then it wouldn't be good.

Fergus: A bit frightening yeah. But why did you stop?

Yoshito: In 1968 I made a solo work. The sound person was Kazuo Ohno. He improvised putting on the music. So every day we practiced in this studio. He would say every time 'it was good today, it was great today.' Then my wife said 'So there are 3 days to go.' She was doing the costume. When I thought there are 3 days to go, I couldn't dance any more. I was free until then but once I thought of 3 days to go, it made me like this … (*gesturing tightness*).

Jacky: Tension …

Yoshito: Yes I became tense.
So I didn't practice anymore. And even on the performance day, I said I wouldn't practice. Then Tatsumi Hijikata came and said 'I want to see'; and he praised a particular part in this dance. Well, because it was improvisation, I didn't understand what it meant when he said this particular part was good.
And the show started
I couldn't move.
I couldn't move at all.
Then I felt empty
I had worked on it for so long (and also spent a lot of money).

It felt so very empty and I thought then that I would try something else and do a normal job! (*General laughter*).

Yoshito: But there was someone who praised the not dancing in a magazine, the writer thought it was somehow pure. That always remained in my heart – 'He didn't move when he couldn't move, he didn't do what other people do.' It was praising my honesty in the moment. Usually, if you can't move, you'll try covering with technique or move or something, but I didn't do that, I was honest. It was a great support later on for someone to have written that about me – I was always thinking about that.

Fergus: So now, how do you feel differently as a dancer than you did when you were very young?

Yoshito: When I started classes with my father, I didn't like it at all. But he taught me to walk this way … or that way (*again demonstrating the walk training*). I came to understand the importance of the exercise. I understand the importance now.

I started class at 13 at Kazuo Ohno's studio and I had my debut at 20 with Tatsumi Hijikata. I was always with Tatsumi Hijikata but I also started going to classical ballet class for 3 or 4 years and also pantomime. Marcel Marceau[9] came to Japan and also Jean-Louis Barrault[10] – I was very moved by this; I wondered how I could move like Marcel Marceau, like this … (*Yoshito exquisitely demonstrates head and torso isolations*) and also from his teacher, Etienne Decroux[11] I learnt exercises to do in front of the mirror every day. Like this and like this …

Fergus: The Decroux system of isolations?

Yoshito: Yes. Pull like this and pull like this (*demonstrating isolation technique*).
I practiced in front of the mirror. I did that for 3 or 4 years.

Jacky: In your 20s?

Yoshito: Yes, and classical ballet

Jacky: Did you find that useful?

Yoshito: I heard Tatsumi Hijikata saying that the form of ballet was beautiful – so I went to do ballet. The core of my training was Butoh with Tatsumi Hijikata and Kazuo Ohno, while also learning the essence of ballet and pantomime.

Jacky: You were drawing on elements from other techniques – mime, classical ballet …

Yoshito: Some of the audience members who saw me dance year after year during that early period realized I was developing and changing 'oh there is a new element in his dance, another blossom has flowered … and there is another new flower …'. That period finished after 7 years – when I was 20–27.

Jacky: And the 17-year period away from dance after that solo performance when you couldn't move – how did that inform your work when you returned to dance?

Yoshito: During the time out from dance I directed plays and opera and that experience made me more objective towards myself. More observant of whom I am.

Fergus: And when you came back to dance that was also when you started to direct your father in his performances?

Yoshito Ohno dancing in Paris, 2006. Photograph permission of Yoshito Ohno

Yoshito: Yes in *Admiring La Argentina*[12] and *My Mother*,[13] directing and also doing the sound.

Fergus: Did you compose any music?

Yoshito: No – I selected and operated the sound – creating sound scores. When I went to Israel, there was a party after the performance in Haifa. Some of the audience members commented that I was also dancing, while doing the sound – they were looking at me. So when we came back and started making *Dead Sea*[14] Kazuo Ohno said 'dance with me.' So I said OK. (*All laugh*)

Jacky: So you started again – and it felt good?

Yoshito: Yes. Tatsumi Hijikata, who was worried about this comeback (I was also worried) gave me three pieces of choreography, and he said 'Chopin has been around for 200 years. Please can you make Butoh continue for 200 years.' I was very surprised because before he had said 'non permanence is beauty' but now he was saying 200 years! (*All laugh*)

Jacky: He was evolving.

Yoshito: Yes. He was evolving.

He left many words.

There are so many surprises.

For example, he said 'technique is a must for a dancer.'

I was surprised. Ahaaaaa …

I think this is valuable for the young generation today.

Jacky: Our book is called *The Wise Body* and it would be interesting to ask you, Yoshito, what you feel you do better now than when you were younger? As a wise body.

Yoshito: How am I better? How am I better?

The younger self is still within me.

That is the most important.

So I felt emptiness and quit Butoh and started a job.

In business, if you do it, money starts coming in.

Making art is more complex, you don't always know the outcome.

They are very different.

So I understood that.

So I understood the meaning of art.

I think that's the difference from when I was younger.

Also when I was young I was hard; Tatsumi Hijikata wanted hard movement … hard hard … grhugggggg. At 13 I started hard modern dance (*does a small routine …*)

Kazuo Ohno was soft. He taught me about softness. Tatsumi Hijikata in 1959 … was hard (*demonstrating 50s style gangster posture. All laugh*).

Different! Very different! Then I stopped.

There was the softness on this side and there was the hardness on this side, but when I came back there was a different kind of softness which has remained with me. It was a different kind of softness from the softness I had before. To come back at 45 with no training the body is hard. The movement is different, it required another kind of softness.

Jacky: Informed by the experience?
Yoshito: Yes
I felt this softness was important.
Jacky: And you understood the meaning of art?
Yoshito: Yes. I felt I must pass this on … I must pass this on.

(After about an hour Yoshito left the studio for 5 minutes and returned wearing his costume – a white shirt and trousers. By this time some of his students had arrived, creating a small audience)

Yoshito: I'd like to show Tatsumi Hijikata's choreography; just talking is not detailed enough.
On the 22nd April I was invited to perform at the 62nd anniversary of the founding of Israel. What is most important is love. Human relationship, putting hands together … like this, is important.

(Yoshito proceeds to perform 4 exquisite dances)

Yoshito is both a dancer and an actor. He distils in shape, pattern, and rhythm what is inside him; he embodies emotion and image and every gesture has meaning and power. He uses minimal voice – but even when silent he speaks to us. Music is important and always supports and frames his dances. There is control and precision – there is line and balance; at times he looks a little vulnerable, squatting down to the floor or kneeling clutching a flower – but he completes the movement and the sense of effort becomes part of the beauty of the dance. He is at 72 very beautiful; his Dad at 103 keeps going, allowing Yoshito the role of the youthful son.

One of the dances is performed with a hand puppet and is extraordinary. The puppet is exactly like Kazuo – frail, long black hair, long fingers, a black robe and make-up. Yoshito's face next to the puppet is so delicately expressive – a sad clown-like creature – and the manipulation of Kazuo is so detailed – the puppet's long hands moving in a gestural port de bras; son and father completely linked in time and space. His father is near the end of his life at home in the house next door – but his spirit has joined us in the studio. The other presence is Elvis Presley whose song 'Can't help falling in love' frames the dance. The difference between life and death is somehow meaningless between these three collaborators. Twice during the evening Yoshito tells us that love is the most important thing.

The tradition of the small informal performance seems to run through Noh, Nihon Buyo and Butoh practice within the context of the private studio. It is a private world of performance gems – and a way of keeping the work close to the core – to the heart, and, when necessary out of the gaze of the market place. We all feel very privileged to have witnessed this performance.

(*Applause!*)

Jacky: We were going to ask you how is dance important to the world?
Yoshito: Why do people dance? Yes I would like to answer (*chuckle*).
Jacky: Maybe it's the only thing that contradicts the real darkness – or balances it?
Yoshito: I didn't understand Hijikata Tatsumi's darkness.
I asked many times but I didn't understand darkness.
For example, like cold, like hunger.
His sister was sold as a geisha.
He always thought about his big sister.
He started growing his hair (he had a shaved head before).
He started saying 'My big sister lives within me.'
If he sits down his sister rises up.
When he goes up, the sister drops down. They are together, like this (*Yoshito demonstrates this imagined dual relationship*).
Sit up, sit down, together?
I still didn't quite understand.
Then he said 'Your dance is dance of light…
If there is too much light, it's blinding'.
Kazuo Ohno and Tatsumi Hijikata are a little bit crazy.
In daily life too much sanity put together becomes also insanity.
The relationship of Tatsumi Hijikata, Kazuo Ohno and I was like this.
Tatsumi Hijikata walked like this (*demonstrating*). Gyuuut … (*chuckles*)
'What is that walk Hijikata san?'
'It's the rice field, it's the rice field, the rice field …
Jabojabojabo (*sound describing water paddle*)
This is my walk and it is different to yours …
You are from Yokohama, a city boy
Concrete! It's different.'
Kazuo Ohno had both sides, so he had a bit of a wider field.

His (Kazuo's) father was a fisher man, who went out to Kamchatka to fish. He went far away to Russia. It's very sad but there was also the war. That's also different.

Kazuo Ohno Studio in Kamihoshikawa, Yokohama, Japan, 27 April 2010

A month after we left Japan Kazuo Ohno died, on June 1st 2010 at the age of 103. It was a great experience and honour to have visited his studio where so much Butoh has been researched and created and to witness the outstanding legacy of his work held so beautifully by his son Yoshito.

Notes

1. Kazuo Ohno (1906–2010): performer, writer and teacher; first studied contemporary dance with Misako Miya, a disciple of Mary Wigman in the mid-1930s and returned to dance after 9 years' military service in 1949 after the war. Received international attention with his performance Admiring *La Argentina* in 1980. Regarded as founder of Butoh with Tatsumi Hijikata.
2. Tatsumi Hijikata: a prominent figure in the Japanese experimental dance scene in the 1960s; along with Kazuo Ohno widely regarded as the founding Father of Butoh. Ohno is regarded as 'the soul of Butoh', while Hijikata is seen as 'the architect of Butoh'. Major collaborator of Ohno's until he died in 1987 at the age of 57.
3. Ankoku Buyo: in the early 1960s, Hijikata used the term Ankoku Buyo (dance of darkness) to describe his dance. He later changed the word buyo, filled with associations of Japanese classical dance, to butoh, a long-discarded word for dance that originally meant European ballroom dancing.
4. *Kinjiki* (1959): Hijikata's controversial adaptation of Yukio Mishima's novel *Forbidden Colours*. It explored the taboo of homosexuality and established Hijikata as an iconoclast.
5. Yukio Mishima (1925–70): renowned author and early supporter of Hijikata and Kasuo Ohono's work. He committed ritual suicide in 1970 provoking a virulent debate between opposing political factions.
6. Tatsuhiko Shibusawa(1928–87): the pen name of Shibusawa Tatsuo, a novelist, art critic and translator of French literature active during the Shōwa period of Japan. His essays about black magic, demonology, and eroticism are popular in Japan.
7. Tōru Takemitsu (1930–96): Japanese composer and writer on aesthetics and music theory. He drew from a wide range of influences, including jazz, popular music, avant-garde procedures and traditional Japanese music, in a harmonic idiom largely derived from the music of Claude Debussy and Olivier Messiaen.
8. Eikoh Hosoe: Japanese photographer and film-maker who emerged in the experimental arts movement of post–World War II Japan. He is known for his psychologically charged images, often exploring subjects such as death, erotic obsession and irrationality. Important collaborator of Hijikata.
9. Marcel Marceau (1923–2007): an internationally acclaimed French actor and mime most famous for his persona as Bip the Clown.
10. Jean-Louis Barrault (1910–94): a French actor, director and mime artist; he studied with Charles Dullin and Étienne Decroux and acted and directed with the Comédie Française.
11. Etienne Decroux (1898–1991): studied at Jacques Copeau's Ecole du Vieux-Colombier, where he saw the beginnings of what was to become his life's obsession – Corporeal Mime. During his long career as a film and theatre actor, he created many pieces, using the human body as the primary means of expression.
12. *Admiring La Argentina*: Kazuo Ohno's great stage comeback performance in 1977 was a tribute to the Spanish dancer La Argentina, Antonia Merce, for whom he had profound admiration. The premier was directed by Hijikata who called it Ohno's first real Butoh performance.

13. *My Mother* (1981): a major work that was a tribute to Kazuo's own Mother – Midori Ohno – a deeply influential figure in his life, directed by Hijikata.
14. *Dead Sea* (premiere 1985 at the Tokyo Butoh Festival): performed by Yoshito with his father and directed by Hijikata before his death in 1986. Inspired by a visit to the Dead Sea during a performance tour of Israel in 1983.

Chapter 6

How Important is Dance? I Think it May be Critical!

Steve Paxton

Steve Paxton in *The Beast*, 2010. Photograph: Julieta Cervantes

Fergus: I am interested in what made you start dancing and what was your attitude to your body before and after you started dancing.

Steve: I think I made the decision to seriously study dancing, because I went to University and found the particular institution in Arizona that I went to educationally inept. Going from high school, I had looked forward to University, where suddenly I would be given the chance to really encounter minds, and thinking and processes and learning of a new order. I had signed up for seventeen courses and at the end of the first term I was depressed - the only thing I had enjoyed was modern dance, which I had done a bit of during high school. I decided well, this has promise.

It took me a long time to admit that I was a dancer. I was with the Merce Cunningham[1] Company, aged 22 or 23, before I said to myself OK, I guess I'm a dancer. Because I held dancers in such high esteem – dancers who were above me seemed super-human and super-spiritual creatures and super-intellectual as well. You had minds like Viola Farber[2] and Carolyn Brown[3] and Cunningham himself and the people around them, which included the whole abstract expressionist painting circle and John Cage[4] and the other musicians and the Living Theatre.[5] This was the kind of pantheon I discovered as I entered the world of the New York arts scene. There was a lot to look up to, so it took me a long time to feel that I was part of it.

But prior to that, I had been tumbling and dancing, so at the point where I decided that I was a dancer, I realized that I had been a dancer all my life. I had been rolling and kicking and jumping and running and playing with a great sense of the interior life of the body, my whole life.

Fergus: Where did that come from, or how did you manage not to lose it?

Steve: I don't know how I managed not to lose it. That's an interesting question. That assumes that people have it and then they lose it. I lived in safe physical surrounds; perhaps my guardians of various sorts – mother, father and people who cared for me – weren't afraid that I be a free person in the world. I came from an area where people weren't afraid of the world. They expected people to get a few knocks, but by and large it didn't have a lot of threats. Children could exist in the same world as old people and adults and teenagers and were comfortable in this world. It wasn't a world that was designed for a specific age group or a specific health group. It was an incredibly benign environment.

Now I don't know what made me interested in the interior rather than the exterior. I remember a little friend of mine showed me how to do cartwheels when I was maybe

6 or 7. She produced a skill that I then tried to learn. In fact she was probably my first teacher, now I think about it. But I enjoyed the feeling of that learning and finally achieving. I enjoyed the first time I put on roller skates and then learnt to roller skate, with all the bumps and scrapes that that required. In a city, I think the adventures tend to be more mental and artistic. The more it gets to be small town or rural, the more it gets to be physical. I've often thought that if I were going to choose dancers for a company, I would go back to Flagstaff, Arizona, 7000 feet in the air, where lungs have to be large and people have to be physical. I'd lock them in a studio and then bring them down to sea level and just blow everybody's minds! (*Laughs*).

Fergus: When you say you were interested in the interior world, what sort of images can you remember?

Steve: The mechanics of moving were interesting to me. Seeing people turn in the movies – you know, those spotless turns on shiny floors with people ending in a flashy pose – Fred and Ginger – and trying it and failing and thinking Uh huh! What do their bodies know that mine doesn't?

But also I was a gymnast, I had done pretty well and enjoyed gymnastics in middle school and when I got to high school I was in a much larger school with a complete gymnastics team with fantastic performers on it, who were doing very well state-wide. Suddenly my vista rose enormously and I was very much at the bottom of this hierarchy and there was something in the spirit of this team – there was a generosity and a pleasantness amongst the guys. And it happened to be a high school which had more people than the whole population of the small town where I moved from – my graduating class was something like 1200 people. I was suddenly in this enormous city of a school, we were the largest high school in the United States at that point.

I started working out with the team and looking round and discovering activities that I'd never even heard of before and seeing people really proficient on apparatus that I'd never seen before. But in the second and subsequent terms my schedule meant that I couldn't take that class, so I started working out at noon, by myself in order to take part in this very pleasant atmosphere of physical activity that I had seen going on. I strove, during my lunch hour, to perfect what I could, which was not very much gymnastics, because there was nobody to spot me and teach me, but I emulated the free exercise kind of thing, because I could do that. I could balance on one leg, I could cartwheel (because my little friend had taught me to cartwheel) and I could stand on my hands long enough to roll out of it before I fell out of it. I made it up and I worked very hard for that whole term and I think the coach was impressed. Finally I was told there was going to be a competition. I competed and I took sixth in the state, with the influence of that great learning environment. So, that somehow affirmed to me that I could work and I could learn and I could achieve. I wasn't first in the state, but I was something in the state, and this was, you know, incredible to me, I was pleased.

Then I went to University and found the University really lacking and I decided: Well, I'm going to try dance. So I announced to my parents that I was seriously going to try dance and, bless their hearts, they didn't say 'Are you out of your mind?' They said, 'Oh, OK.' They left it totally up to me to get out of town and set myself up in New York, and when I say totally, I mean no financial aid, no advice, no bus ticket, no clothes, no suitcase, no anything.

But one of my dance teachers was a nun who was one of two Graham teachers in Tucson at that point who were in association. I had been studying with both of them and performing with both of them and somewhat touring with both of them, especially the nun, because the convent had schools elsewhere that we could get to in the VW bus and drive to and do a little performance and drive back. That was the touring I was talking about. And they had a convent on Long Island and they were driving there in the spring. So I was employed as a driver and that's how I got East.

And then I had written to the American Dance Festival[6] for a scholarship, but received no answer. It was not far from the convent, however, and I just walked in and said: 'Well, Yes or No? I haven't received an answer.' And they said: 'Oh, we were just getting the answers out, and it looks like you're in.' And so I went to the American Dance Festival that summer and started serious training, and it was very good training, I think. I've gone back to the American Dance Festival and it's still good training. It was interesting then and it's fascinating now. American Dance Festival suddenly put me into three technical classes, a composition class, rhythm studies and seeing loads of performances, including Graham, Humphrey, Limón, Pearl Lang, Cunningham, Paul Taylor[7] – lots of performances and my scholarship meant that I was working backstage, so I was watching all the rehearsals of those performances. There was a schedule of other performances where I wasn't working, so I would sneak in to watch those as well. It was a crash course in modern dance.

Fergus: How long does it last?

Steve: It lasts 6 weeks, and it gets you into shape, so that when you go into the city it's not daunting to take a class a day. I went to the city and got a job and got a place to stay and took a class a day. And then it got to be a class and a rehearsal or two rehearsals a day, so I was up to midnight or 1 o'clock in the morning and then getting home and then getting up and going to work and working all day and taking class at night. I did that for a year. Then I quit my job taking documents between Rockefeller Institute and Wall Street. The only job I ever had! And I went back to Connecticut College, to the American Dance Festival the next summer. This time I'd had enough training that I could be used by a slightly higher level of choreographer, I wasn't just a student. The year after that, I started my own company and did children's performances in summer camps. I got hold of a little old rusty car and got some props together and made a dreadful show and toured it around to summer camps.

Fergus: On your own?

Steve: With three other people. I didn't like it much, but it was a great education in some ways. It was sort of a failure but it was a great education in the logistics of the whole thing. There was another aspect – there was something called the Merry-Go-Rounders, which was again for children and was very well organized and had a repertoire; you came in and learned the dances and performed them for several thousand children, sometimes. We took it around to schools and did it there – we did it anywhere. It was a lot of performance training.

Fergus: Another question I have is: how important is dance?

Steve: Well, I'm still working on that one. I think the arts seem to concentrate in urban areas and that they somewhat take the place of nature, the nature that gets squeezed out by the concentration of people. I mean if you're a person throwing yourself around the landscape, I think you get all the same physical training, maybe even more, just coping with the landscape, the climbing and swinging and running and walking and lifting that you do within a landscape. In the city you don't have to do that.

So, how important is dance to those people living in the city? I think it provides a model for the body, which means the body is not encapsulated only by what the urban architectural situation is, which is really minimal and degrades the body to a very simplified version of what it could be. Potential is minimized. Where I live in the country, I don't sense that dance is so necessary except as an alternative to the work that people are doing – it's like a natural kind of chiropractic,[8] or as a natural kind of exuberant exercise that doesn't require that you achieve anything, so you are just lifting the body's own weights and working its levers and things like that, to keep it from ageing too fast and being too degraded by the work.

I notice that a lot of dance from Africa, for instance, is the work that they do, or the hunting, but taken into a sort of stylized form, so the actions are practised, but not with the real game or with the real digging involved, still using the same digging sticks but using them as a rhythmic instrument and so the effort is taken to a different level. I think that's probably really good for their bodies – the movements they have to do are practised not only under the loads and stresses that are normally done, but are taken into rhythm and pleasure; the muscles are given a different message – they are expressing something instead of achieving something. I think that psychological difference probably enhances life … How important is dance? I think it might be critical!

Only certain senses are really needed in the city and a lot of the senses seem to be shut down – you shut down to the noise, you select only a few avenues for the senses that are the appropriate ones, the necessary ones. Vision gets much used. Hearing gets much shut down, except when you want to hear an announcement or something.

Fergus: Don't you think vision does get shut off as well? I notice that on tubes nobody's looking at anybody. I try to keep my attention out and look around me …

Steve: You do look, but it isn't the same as looking in a forest, where you're looking three-dimensionally, at much greater depth, with much greater subtlety of colour. Say you're looking for an animal and they're camouflaged and they're extraordinarily quiet, and their senses are much greater so you really have to be paying attention to the wind and the forest floor tracks and the weather and how far you are from things and keeping the spatial coordinates, maybe for miles. And walking around trees and around swamps and still trying to keep on track. I didn't travel vast distances in New York. I lived in an area where I could walk to pretty much anything I was going to do. It was good walk. It was, however, on concrete and the people were obstacles to be ignored and avoided, more than greeted or talked to or exchanged with along the way. I lived in some of the poorest areas of the city, so I realized at a certain point that I was putting out a lot of energy to ignore things, to not look at the drunks in doorways to not notice the dog shit and vomit and things like that that I was avoiding. To ignore the smells of car pollution and excrement and to not feel things for the people I was looking at. To not hear the sounds of honking and screeching and collisions and revving of engines – those weren't necessary things to pick up on.

And then I moved to the country and I felt what happened to me – quite a shocking thing. Suddenly it was worth really getting into smell, because there were some delicious things to smell, depending which way the air was blowing; and it was worth keeping my eyes open because it might be that I was on the periphery of the fields where I could watch what the horses were doing or watch the wind across the grasses or watch the colours change through the seasons; and the plants, wondering what they were and if they were edible and beginning to eat them and to name them and explore them and research them. I realized that many things around me were not only edible but were superior to things I could grow. The area where I live has a very long winter, but in the short summer it is really benign. I can walk for miles through the woods bare-footed – the floor of the forest is soft and pleasant to walk on and aside from stubbing your toe, not much can happen. There are no animals that bother you. There are no poisonous snakes or insects or plants. And loads of stuff is not only edible but desirable – the mushrooms, and all around the gardens, the things that grow there, the weeds, are better than the vegetables. Lambsquarters is an incredible plant. You can put it in a salad and you can dry it and put it in your soups – it's really high protein, sort of like a spinach, but superior to that. It's related to quinoa, the Peruvian plant that sustained the Aztecs. Its seeds are a grain and you can grind them to make bread. This is just a weed. Other naturals might have roots which are medicinal and highly nutritious, and in each season the leaves and the seeds and the flowers are edible. Suddenly the landscape starts to look like dinner! In the city you don't find that at all. That was the difference.

I also, beyond dance, studied Yoga and Aikido[9] and T'ai Chi.[10]

Steve Paxton outside the studio he shares with Lisa Nelson in Vermont, US, 2005. Photograph: Jacky Lansley

Fergus: Was this before, after, or what?

Steve: OK. It was gymnastics, modern dance, ballet, Yoga, Aikido, T'ai Chi, in that order. So the movement and the positions of the body started to look a bit like that landscape I was mentioning. Instead of the body being a vehicle for clothes, an occupier of furniture and cars and tubes, suddenly these positions started to be asanas, they started to be energy expressions in a different way than I had experienced the body before, so the body started to look like a self-repairing citadel … yeah, citadel. Something like a city, an enclosed unit where many parts interrelate in ways to keep themselves going. And not only the physical aspects of things – I mean it started off just being loads of dancing – but the energetic, spiritual and imagistic aspects of the body as well, all interlinked. It's a microcosm of the culture in a way.

Fergus: What are you performing at the moment?

Steve: I'm performing a structured improvisation to the English Suites by Johann Sebastian Bach. And it's all I'm doing. I absolutely don't see any reason, as long as I'm working on one structured improvisation, to change the music. It was true of the previous solo that I made, which was to the entire Goldberg Variations by Bach, played by Glenn Gould.[11] I like Glenn Gould because he's such a percussionist and I like Bach because he's such a trickster, because he's not afraid to be boring and because he also really soars. He plays the lulls and stimulations in a very interesting way.

Fergus: How long are the English Suites?

Steve: They're very long. I don't use the complete English Suites; I do from eight to twenty, twenty-two sometimes. It depends on what I'm asked to do. Sometimes I'm asked to do 8 minutes, sometimes I'm asked to do a programme. The Goldberg was 45 minutes and I got in shape for that by using vibration – just simply trying to vibrate my body and using the vibration to spring into larger movement – as the improvisational theme of what I was doing and that got me into such good shape that I then could go on to 45 minutes with movement that wasn't vibrational. I don't think I could vibrate for 45 minutes. That vibrational solo was probably 10 minutes and it really took everything out of me! I once had to do it twice of an evening, for two different shows and I came out of there as tired as … I mean a full Cunningham concert never took as much out of me as that vibration solo.

Fergus: What does it mean, vibration?

Steve: Shaking. Shaking all my bits and pieces, every category of my body and limbs that I could get going at once. Head, tail. Arms, legs, hands, fingers and tensions all over the body. It's just very hard to breathe through all of that.

Fergus: I've just remembered seeing you do some very wild shaking at one of the Dartington Festivals.[12]

Steve: I might have done it there. I became very interested in tiny units of movement and that got me into the vibrations. Small, sharp changes. That's what worked so well with the way Gould plays, because he's so fast. Gould's ten fingers against my body … what those ten fingers are doing, of course, is several different lines of music at once and to try to do the same thing with my body was a good education, a real test to try to maintain connections with the different strands of the Bach.

Fergus: But what you're doing now is not based on vibrations?

Steve: No. After I had done the Goldberg for about 6 or 7 years, I thought, how do I get out of this, because every new invention that goes into it just becomes the Goldberg variations, because it's improvised, not doing the same thing from night to night. It's just sucking me dry. How do I get out of this? How do I stop it? I decided to change the music to find a principle to work with again. Like the shaking. And the new principle is spirals. 'Spirals' are based on the ground, and the base of the spiral has the potential to rotate a little bit, to twist – it's as though you take an X and you put that X standing up on the ground and the X has ankles and feet and those feet can roll on the floor and then the same thing happens in the hips – where I'm not using the rotational possibilities to control the thighs, as you do in turn-out, but rather to affect the torso. The arms are used rather as you do in Aikido, extending through the little finger and ring finger. With those kinds of principles, the Aikido arm, when you extend it forward as in the Aikido roll, means your little finger is leading forward in space – if you extend that stretch in reverse, away from the little finger and up the arm and down the back, it gets into that big elastic area in the lumbar region. So I'm pulling the big lines of tendon down there in the lumbar, outward with the arm and then also pulling them downwards with the rotation forward and down of the pelvis. So I'm treating lumbar tendons as a trampoline and I'm tensing in various ways. So that's the physiology of the current improvisation.

Fergus: How many improvising dancers are there in the world? There are so few.

Steve: I'm not sure there can be a lot of them. Improvisation is something everybody does every day. It's so ordinary it's hard to see. It's hard to know you're doing it. You think you have a plan – you don't realize how much of that plan you have to improvise. You think about the goal and the steps you know are necessary to get there, but there are steps in between steps and you don't consider all of those, you don't need to, your body just does it. So it's hard to think about it. It's hard to notice it. It's hard to realize just how basic it is. So I would say, in a funny way, everybody's involved in improvisation, but they don't notice it. And the ones who really are noticing that and are trying to get rid of the things that make it look formal, because they want to see what improvisation looks like, are not so many, because it's a very wild area.

If you say the word 'improvisation', you're generalizing, always. Whereas if you talk about a known and specific technique, then you can get more and more specific. You can bring the conscious brain more and more into it and plan the sequences or design the connections, as between media, and the conscious brain is very comfortable with that, because the conscious brain is after all what we know we know. And so you build a better ladder, or better lines of communication between different parts of the conscious brain and you get a real sense of accomplishment in the working of the conscious brain itself.

But in improvisation you're trying to do another thing. You're trying to lay that massive tool, which knows itself, aside. You're trying to acknowledge that the body has an innate something that you don't know, and that you can't know. You can't know what it's going to be. You're trying to acknowledge that you can't know something and this is a real catch-22 for the brain. This is a conundrum. I don't know how I came to trust it ... I don't know how I got that little mental trick, to lay aside the conscious brain – it's a little bit like learning how to whistle, you couldn't describe how you do it, you just ... (*whistles*)

Fergus: How do you find your body? How's it doing, nowadays?

Steve: Rationally, I know that it's changed considerably from when I started dancing in the fifties! But it still feels the same. Its current interesting developments are that it's balancing better. It's balancing much better. It's turning more accurately, with more precision in the balance of the turn and more feeling of the suspension in the momentum of the turn. It's almost as though its geometry is clearer to me, and that gives me a whole new potential. It's still capable technically of doing many things. I don't have the endurance I used to do, but I think a lot of that may have to do with smoking. Mind you, I've only stopped doing a 45-minute solo for a couple of years so I haven't tested it to that degree, lately.

I've learned how to stretch. I learned how to stretch when I was 45 – before that I resisted proper stretching. I think it was just lack of concept. I certainly didn't understand the real concept of letting the muscle release.

Fergus: Not through Yoga?

Steve: I think it took Yoga a long time to get the message through to a young, tight, muscle-bound guy. I do think it was Yoga and T'ai Chi that allowed that to happen, finally. And illness. One time I was ill on tour and I couldn't leave the tour without disabling the company, so I had to dance while being very weak and I suddenly realized I could do everything I had to do, I just wasn't doing it with the sproinginess [*sic*] I had been investing the movement with before. And that that sproinginess was not necessary; and then the muscles began to learn to release. But it was a long and gradual process, especially in the hamstrings and other places where men are traditionally rather tight. It took me a very long time to achieve. Now I love it. Before, it was extremely painful, because I was just doing it wrong. I presume that's what happened. One never knows, you know. One does not know whether the changes are progress or degeneration or just change. But internally, and for myself as a sensing of my own body, I can't tell the difference, I might as well still be 15. It's still that kind of eternal me, trying to move. I remember, when I was starting to study dance, I told myself, When I get old I must remember that it was never easy, so that when it's hard when I'm old, I won't think it's only difficult because I'm old! I'm young now, and this is really hard! And it's just been different things that were difficult. The things that are difficult now are not the things that were difficult then. All in all, I'm quite surprised to still be dancing. I thought you stopped at 35 if you had any integrity. Possibly that's true, I don't know!

But anyway, I'm 20 years on, past that, and it's been a really interesting 20 years, because I feel like I'm still discovering systems in the body that I hadn't noticed before, and new ideas to pursue. I've noticed that I'm pursuing backwards towards classicism. Right now what I'm doing looks very balletic to me. I'm very interested in the spirals of the body and I keep getting into attitudes and my arms keep going into proper balletic positions. Dance has kept my body very healthy. I haven't had any hip replacements! Really the hardest thing about dance has been the travelling, and trying to eat properly, things like that, just the obvious basics of it all.

Fergus: So you don't carry chronic injuries?

Steve: No. Oh, wait. There was one, and it disabled me quite a bit, for a couple of years. It was in my piraformis muscle that goes from the sacrum to the hip, under the buttocks; I had a trauma which made me think I had arthritis in my left hip. It was rather painful and very worrying to someone who hasn't had that much trouble with my body and it eventually was solved with massage. It was caused by a vaccination, I think. You know those vaccinations you get to go to the tropics where you have a load of poisons shot into your buttock to keep you from getting something unmentionable. I still have a kind of nodule in that muscle which I think is the actual site where the poison was injected.

Fergus: And what do you do to care for yourself in a physical way?

Steve: I work in the landscape. I work on a farm.

Fergus: And do you literally grind things and shift earth and that sort of thing?

Steve: I do as much as possible by hand – that is pulling a wagon by hand, like a Chinese peasant. Lifting, pushing, shovelling. I grow a lot of earth, I compost and move the earth with that wagon and dump it into the beds and remove the old earth and re-compost it, so I'm doing a lot of that kind of thing, working with earth. The whole thing about gardening, bending over and having the head lower than the waist – which is never done in Bali, I found : it is somehow considered obscene to have the head lower than the pelvis – but I find it quite good for me to be bending over, the stretch in the back, the change for the heart from pumping up to the head to pumping down to the head, the stretch in the back of the legs, the work with the hands, the pulling actions and the whole thing of gathering, the whole thing of sorting, all of that.

Fergus: Does squatting come in there at all?

Steve: Squatting, kneeling. Yes. Sometimes I work in a squatting position until my back muscles are just tingling with fatigue, really getting pins and needles from not having a contraction. Yes, really serious long-term stressing of certain muscles. And then the relief from that. Or just lying down, right there beside the garden and taking a rest! I like to rest a lot. I have a few apple trees, so I'm climbing a lot in the pruning and stuff like that. A lot of carrying, which includes firewood, so I'm doing it several times a day for a couple of different stoves.

So that's the basic sub-structure of it all. When I dance, then, I work to relieve the stresses that the work, with all its variations, has caused, which means a lot

Steve Paxton. Photograph: © Peter Nellhaus

of working with the body's own masses – feeling the massiveness of a leg or an arm or the head or the torso, the upper torso versus the lower torso – and looking for structures. The structure which I'm working with now (spirals) comes out of contact improvisation, which I'm still doing, however many years later – it started in '72 – and I like contact improvisation for putting my body into so many different positions, just that simple fact of it, plus relating to somebody else's unpredictability, so it seems to keep the reflexes stimulated. Plus the senses and how they're stimulated – what kind of difference there is between laying the eyes right in the skull as you're moving, so you're still sensing but you're not directing the movement with the eyes, or the eyes aren't important except as ancillary senses. But the touch and the whole kinetic knowledge become paramount. So you're switching the hierarchy of the senses. And you change the hierarchy of the body and its weight-bearing too. Because it isn't just your buttocks and legs and knees and palms that take weight, which is the normal few places that we work with, but every place on the body has to become the connection to the earth, which means it's a kind of fulcrum from which the body works in different ways, so every part of the surface gets used that way and the nerves which connect through to the skeleton and to the organs – that primary relationship to gravity and surface is transmitted to the brain through different parts of surface.

And then what I'm doing with my forebrain seems to be looking for these structures, and the structures are ever so much simpler than the things I've just been talking about, and I begin to realize that the dance techniques that I've been trying to learn and to study, especially at the beginning, weren't sophisticated systems, they were in fact simplified systems. Once I understood that, I wasn't intimidated to try to make work. I thought, well, I can simplify something – I don't know if I can make it more complex than it already is, but I can certainly understand a simpler version of it …

I mean how many possibilities do you need to make a system that's more complex than we can comprehend? It takes about three or four twists of any idea and it's beyond me. Not for the chess genius, perhaps, but for the average person like myself – how many moves ahead can I see in a game? Not very many. And chess itself is a simplification. It's just a game and look what it can do. My game, actually, to show you something about my brain, is Chinese checkers, as opposed to chess. A very simple game in which competition is not about gaining the other person's men, it's about moving and efficiency. That's the only game I play. I just decided that the other games were just too complex for me! I like the kind of complexity which happens in Chinese checkers, which is more about a very simple field and very simple actions, and just trying to figure out what the system is that makes a winning strategy.

Fergus: I have played Go. The board is so big and the possibilities seem so many in Go. It's quite a frightening game.

Steve: A frightening game, and you have to allow for these switching of potentials – you surround them and then they surround you... and sometimes you have to let them surround you so that you can surround them and you have to work out how many surrounds there are, so that you'll end up ahead of the game. To translate that into movement, I've noticed that one of the problems that people have with some of the simple rolling training exercises that I use is that they push against the floor with their hand, and in that push leave their hand behind and lose the form that they are trying to keep. So that they lose the roll in order to effect the roll. Whereas if they tried to achieve that same thing by extension through that same hand in the direction the roll is going, for instance – I'm talking about a spiral roll here – then they wouldn't lose the form and they wouldn't leave that weight mass behind that they use to push with to get their torso to change and they would have the potential always ahead of them, to draw from. That weight mass would be ahead of them, to draw their torso forward as opposed to leaving the weight mass behind. In other words, they block themselves. And once I saw that, I thought, well actually, we block ourselves all the time. The analogy just goes through our whole system.

Fergus: It's what I feel about trying to play Irish tunes on a whistle. I grew up playing classical tunes on a recorder from the music, and that process continually blocks the possibility of playing easily on a whistle, where playing by ear is paramount. These blocks are laid into you; they serve some purpose, but they are blocks, too.

Steve: Isn't that the way! In improvisation, there is this idea that it's a freedom that you're going toward, but I don't think there is such a thing as freedom. I think you can be free from something, but you're always involved in some system, and it has its own rules. And so the idea of freedom is a little bit different than I thought it was – it's freedom from, but not freedom from everything. It's only freedom from a few things, or freedom from the last thing. You can leave some place, but you're always someplace else.

London, UK, 6 January 1995

Notes

1. Merce Cunningham (1919–2009): US dancer and choreographer who was at the forefront of the American avant-garde for more than 50 years. Throughout much of his life, Cunningham was considered one of the greatest creative forces in American dance. He is also notable for his frequent collaborations with artists of other disciplines, including musicians John Cage and David Tudor, artists Robert Rauschenberg and Bruce Nauman, designer Romeo Gigli, and architect Benedetta Tagliabue.
2. Viola Farber: dancer, choreographer and teacher and founder member of the Cunningham company 1953–65.
3. Carolyn Brown: founder member of the Cunningham company.

4. John Cage (1912–92): an American composer, philosopher and poet. A pioneer of chance music, electronic music and non-standard use of musical instruments; Cage was one of the leading figures of the post-war avant-garde and one of the most influential American composers of the twentieth century. He was also instrumental in the development of modern dance, mostly through his association with choreographer Merce Cunningham.

5. The Living Theatre: founded in 1947 as an imaginative alternative to the commercial theatre by Judith Malina and Julian Beck and has influenced theatre the world over. During the 1950s and early 1960s in New York, The Living Theatre pioneered the unconventional staging of poetic drama by writers such as Gertrude Stein, William Carlos Williams, Paul Goodman, Kenneth Rexroth, John Ashbery, Cocteau, Lorca, Brecht and Pirandello.

6. The American Dance Festival: a summer festival of modern dance performances and training, currently held at Duke University and the Durham Performing Arts Center in Durham, North Carolina.

7. [Martha] Graham, [Doris] Humphrey, [José] Limón, Pearl Lang, [Merce] Cunningham, Paul Taylor: all leading US modern dance artists of the time.

8. Chiropractic: a health care discipline that emphasizes diagnosis, treatment and prevention of mechanical disorders of the musculoskeletal system, especially the spine, under the hypothesis that these disorders affect general health via the nervous system.

9. Aikido: a Japanese martial art developed by Morihei Ueshiba (1883–1969) as a synthesis of his martial studies, philosophy and religious beliefs. Ueshiba's goal was to create an art that practitioners could use to defend themselves while also protecting their attacker from injury.

10. T'ai Chi Chuan: an internal Chinese martial art practised for both its defense training and its health benefits. Some of T'ai Chi Chuan's training forms are especially known for being practised at what most people categorize as a slow pace.

11. Glenn Herbert Gould (1932–82): Canadian pianist who became one of the best-known and most celebrated classical pianists of the twentieth century. He was particularly renowned as an interpreter of the keyboard music of Johann Sebastian Bach.

12. Dartington Festivals: in the 1970s and 1980s, Dartington College of Arts in Devon, United Kingdom, hosted a series of annual dance festivals, instigated by Mary Fulkerson (then head of dance at Dartington), which brought together many of the leading artists and teachers in United Kingdom, United States and European new and experimental dance.

Chapter 7

Lines of Experience

Jacky Lansley

Jacky Lansley as The Tap Dancer in the film *The Gold Diggers*, Director Sally Potter, 1981. Photograph: Babette Mangolte.

Fergus: When and how did you start to dance?

Jacky: I boarded at a performing arts school in London, The Grandison College, from the age of 8–16 where I studied a whole range of techniques – ballet, tap, ballroom dance, modern dance, singing, folk dance, acting and piano. I remember in my first ballet class I had to skip and gallop, the stuff I had been doing in the playground, and I thought 'I can do this' – it was a good beginning! I was a very busy child and probably didn't have enough time for other areas of development, particularly as an adolescent and so I had to do some of that catching up later on as a young adult – a process which began in earnest when I became a student at The Place[1] (a period which included working with Strider[2] and Richard Alston[3]) after I had left the Royal Ballet Company. Although I had a very intense and demanding early training, I managed to maintain quite a free athleticism, which I think did stay with me and which I always enjoyed. The ballet training didn't tighten me up as it can do; but then of course I chose to let a lot of that tension go from a very early age, and explore contemporary and release techniques and develop as a choreographer. So for a long time I've been working on alternatives.

Fergus: How do you feel differently now from when you were a very young performer?

Jacky: Emotional range can be absent in your dancing and performing if you haven't had time to develop parts of yourself. And so that's how I feel different. I feel that my body is now more experienced, and that has a kind of presence in performance. I have been able to unravel more pieces of myself which is an emotional as well as physical process, isn't it? I think that if one has done a lot of muscular training as a child it can lead to a kind of tightness in which parts of yourself – both your physical and emotional self – can be held; if you work to release those restrictions you free up energy and creativity.

Fergus: What performance experiences have you enjoyed most?

Jacky: The dancing experiences when I felt very physically powerful and able to enjoy the freedom that gave me; dancing from a position of being very physically strong – being right up on top of it. This enables one to transcend the technique and experience, literally, a sense of flying. I feel I've had that experience sometimes when dancing. This powerful visceral quality is different from creating a very particular aesthetic image demanded by, for example, something like *Les Sylphides*,[4] which I think I probably found quite hard as a very young ballet dancer. It was a demanding discipline for me having to create a very exact stylistic image, unless I completely understood the cultural and aesthetic background to it, which we were not always given – that part of my training and development came later within another context. Although I must here give credit to my childhood ballet teacher Jean Campbell (the skipping and galloping) – she instilled in me some very basic and useful ideas about line, perspective and subtlety. She didn't encourage crude high legs which distort the line; there was something really quite cultured and subtle about her teaching which conveyed the importance of presentation and style alongside technique. However, being thrown in at the deep end I found it very difficult, for example in the Royal Ballet Company, when Leonide Massine[5] tried to get me to perform a very specific physical character, a very small role in his ballet *La Boutique Fantasque*.[6] I had to make an entrance with an escort in front of the front drop during the scene change and he wanted the geste and character absolutely exact. I sensed it was a very valuable experience and that I was learning my craft, but it was quite hard and Massine was quite terrifying! That was a different kind of experience from enjoying the sheer physicality of movement and dance.

Later when I became involved in very visual work within a performance art context, I remembered my experience with Massine and understood more clearly the rich background to his work and its complex interdisciplinary influences (Massine first trained as an actor, you know). And I began to enjoy and really take on board the process of adapting my dance and theatrical skills and placing them within a different, aesthetic environment. I started to enjoy the wit and humour of deconstructing and playing with images, and using my physical expertise to develop that; different pleasures came into performance for me.

Fergus: Can you talk about some of your specific performance art experiences?

Jacky: After leaving The Place in 1974 I created Limited Dance Company with Sally Potter,[7] who had also been a student at The Place. The name, Limited Dance Company, illustrated the paradox in our work for although we related to theatrical and dance traditions we were not part of a mainstream of dance activity or even the fringe. Skilled physical performance was simply one of the elements in works such as *Brief Encounter*[8] and *Mounting*[9] which were primarily image based, and used formal strategies such as repetition, juxtaposition and collage, bringing the work closer to the category of performance art than to any other.

During this phase the work became more cerebral, more conceptual, and I didn't as often experience the sheer physical pleasures of dancing. There were some joyous and extraordinary site-specific moments like walking out of a loch in the west of Scotland in full evening dress with Sally;[10] choreographing a chorus of

Jacky Lansley (on right) with Rose English in *Park Cafeteria* by Limited Dance Company, at the Serpentine Gallery, London, 1975. Photograph: Geoff White

40 borrowed dogs at Kansas City Art Institute; or inhabiting The Serpentine Gallery[11] for a week with five women artists, some old clothes, a piano and a couple of fake guns in *Park Cafeteria*. It was a different kind of enjoyment in performance – the enjoyment of taking risks and feeling like you were participating in something that was part of wider political and cultural changes. We considered everything around the event, how it was marketed, what was written about it, the wider social and historical function and meaning of the spaces we were in – all of which could become part of the performance 'text'.

Within this 'limited dance' context, as a performer I sometimes felt a bit like an exhibit – which is a paradox, as many of the images were concerned with questioning oppressive representations of women. However I began to understand that these feelings were integral to the work as we challenged stereotypes – spent time with them, 'felt' them – and unravelled our personal histories and experience. This period was a crucial part of my training and development as an artist and the question of how to embody visual language and imagery has become central to my choreographic practice and teaching. Limited Dance Company's work was ground breaking and influenced much that followed.

Around this time I began to feel that I needed to integrate what I had been learning in the world of performance art with work that was more movement based, which is why I made a decision to shift focus and became part of the X6 Collective[12] from which the UK New Dance movement primarily emerged. At X6 Dance Space I made many studio and site-specific pieces in the surrounding docklands inspired by minimalist traditions where everything and anything could be used as artistic material; such as *Dance Object*[13] and *Dancing Ledge* (with Rose English[14] who had also worked with Limited Dance Company) in which a crowd of people did everything they could to create distractions and interruptions while Rose and I persisted in a strange and quiet duet wearing anoraks over gold leotards.

Fergus: In the 80s you began to work as a choreographer and movement director in theatre. How did this come about?

Jacky: The Women's Playhouse Trust[16] asked me to choreograph a production of Aphra Behn's[16] *The Lucky Chance* at The Royal Court Theatre;[17] it was a great, and successful, experience, and it was the first of a wave of projects and collaborations I did within the theatre. There are necessarily discrete approaches within theatre and dance – particularly in preparation and training work; but within the creative process I have not found this and have spent a lot of time blurring boundaries. The best actors, I have found, have usually been very physically aware people who dance at some level; and the most interesting dance, for me, has usually had a sense of total theatre about it. Age is part of this, in that there is something inherently 'theatrical' about the older body; it displays more narratives, more tales – and is naturally more colourful because it is experienced.

There tends to be a polarization between theatre and dance, acting and dancing in the West doesn't there? I had the opportunity to work with the Russian theatre director Yuri Lyubimov[18] on his production of *The Possessed* at The Almeida Theatre in London in the 1980s. He was fearless in his eclectic use of physical language and working from the 'outside in' (sometimes you just have to try it rather than discuss it!) He recognized my interdisciplinary approach and made full use of it, often describing it as Meyerholdian – he had himself worked with Meyerhold[19] in the 1920s. It was very affirming to have these influences recognized – my Massine experience for example – and made me feel part of a much larger historical theatrical community. Lyubimov was obsessed with movement and dance; I think he would have liked to make the whole piece as a kind of macabre ballet without any words at all, which was refreshing within that quite establishment UK theatre context. I built on this experience with my project *The Breath of Kings*[20] where I worked with text from Shakespeare's Richard II and explored finding a physical vocabulary that would match the complexity of the text. Richard II, played as a woman, was a powerful role for me to perform and placed great demands on me as a 'speaking dancer'.

Returning to the discussion of age, one of the very liberating aspects of working in theatre with actors is that it stops being such an issue in the same way. Actors of all ages can have very lively careers, as it is their job to portray human beings at all stages in their lives. For an actor to call themselves a dancer – to take that on – can be liberating in a different way. It can provide a nurturing commitment to the body, which we need to do any kind of performance. I feel that all actors could think of themselves as dancers and perhaps all dancers should think of themselves as actors. Think back to the wonderful spectacle of Robert Helpmann[21] performing both *Hamlet* (the play) and Siegfried from *Swan Lake* the ballet. For a performer to have had that range of skill – whatever you think about the success of his performances – is extraordinary.

Fergus: Were you still exploring this relationship between dance and theatre during your 'Stravinsky phase' when you made *Bird* and *L'Autre*?

Jacky: Yes I think I was. *L'Autre*[22] was a radical look at Fokine's *Petrouchka*,[23] and as a consequence of exploring this ballet I became interested in the great actor-dancer Vaslav Nijinsky[24] who first performed the role. Like Helpmann, he seems to have had an amazing range, able to perform both burlesque character roles and classical male leads and to appear both beautiful and grotesque – a range not often, if ever, permitted to women performers. The role of Petrouchka offers a brilliant opportunity to a performer, to explore very precisely the idea of the actor-dancer, and express an extraordinary character through dance; and so I decided to borrow this great male role.

Fergus: Did you use the original choreography?

Jacky: I studied Fokine's[25] choreography very closely (as you and I studied the source

Jacky Lansley in *L'Autre*, 1998. Photograph: Hugo Glendinning

material when we were researching our radical deconstruction *I, Giselle*[26]), and was fascinated how careful I had to be in order to justify my own changes to Fokine's choreography. The character's physicality is very precise and the ballet's pathos and meaning is very distilled within its dance, music and design. I found myself respecting and wanting to inhabit the original choreography, while adapting the structure to a dialogue between the two characters in my version – Petrouchka and The Pianist. I trained hard for 9 months to prepare for the role but found it to be one of the most demanding dances I have ever performed, both emotionally and physically. The character combines weight and substance with the ability of the manipulated puppet to contort and 'fly'. This creature – L'Autre – who could be male or female, explores the full range of human emotion. For a performer it is an amazing challenge and although it placed a lot of demands on my body – I was in my late 40s at the time – it was another great male role to borrow and explore.

Then around 1998 my involvement with Stravinsky's music drew me to another Fokine ballet – *The Firebird* – which I explored through different forms for some years in performance works such *Les Diables*[27] and *Bird*[28], and in 2006 I made a short film *The Life Class*[29] which continued to look at the same themes, and in which I worked with the actress Kathryn Pogson[30] who played 'Bird', and with the actor Vincent Ebrahim[31] who played 'Vaslav'. As a result of all this work involving dancers and actors, I became inspired to develop and organize methods of training for the actor-dancer. I have always been interested in the work of finding a voice for dance, through the practice of the 'speaking dancer' and also socially and politically through my writing and teaching. When I was about 11 years old at theatre school I was asked if I wanted to be an actor or a dancer; I didn't want to choose, and I still don't, in a way. The struggle to find coherence between the two – the voice and the body – which are so strangely divided within our culture, has remained important to me.

Fergus: Could you talk about your current work, training and focus?

Jacky: In 2002 I opened my own studio in East London which I called the Dance Research Studio. From here I began a new phase of work which has returned to a much deeper relationship with movement and with music in a sequence of works exploring landscape and emotional embodiment. It was extraordinary to me that having a home, a studio of my own, brought about this shift of focus in works such as *Holding Space*,[32] *View from the Shore*,[33] *Standing Stones*[34] and most recently *Guests*.[35] An extended visit to the States in 2005 to work again with Bonnie Bainbridge Cohen at the School of Body Mind Centering was also hugely nourishing to me as a teacher and performer.

Making my work over the last 8 years or so has involved a process with several dancers and actors with whom I have built a rich and continuing working relationship. I have not performed in these pieces, but the language mostly comes from my own research and improvised explorations which the performers inhabit and make their own, a process we call the choreographic exchange. I have not stopped working physically in the studio, but I haven't performed for a while (with the exception of *Who Became Those*, a short film that you and I made last year as a tribute to the radical musician Paul Burwell[36]), and I am having to find a new starting place, again, as I work on a solo for myself which will be part of a larger piece in dialogue with Bach's *The Six Cello Suites* which I have been developing slowly over 2 years. The music will be the major inspiration for this solo, but also I find myself drawn to images of Noh theatre[37] which I saw a lot in Japan this year, particularly slow walking.

It may appear that this phase of work is very different from my previous work, but I don't feel that I have abandoned interdisciplinarity – I think it is all still there, but more distilled; my eclectic years of experimentation have given me, I think, a breadth and confidence to be boldly minimal. My music choices would seem to refer back to an early classical training, although I feel the solo instrumental voices of the piano, cello or clarinet in Schubert, Mozart or Bach's music are timeless, giving one a context that is spacious and, in a way, free from contemporary buzz. It is not work that I could have attempted 30 years ago – as my performing over the next years will be very different too.

Also my research into the idea of the speaking dancer has matured into a modular programme – The Speaking Dancer: Interdisciplinary Performance Training (SDIPT) – which offers a space for professional practitioners of any age to concentrate on themselves as performers and explore my training themes around emotional embodiment, sounding dance and the inhabiting of visual image.

Fergus: How important is dance?

Jacky: This year I was in Japan for 6 weeks on a research trip and I had the opportunity to witness some extraordinary solo dance performances mostly in private studios; some of which made me weep with pleasure: A Nihon Buyo[38] version of Pavlova's *Dying Swan*[39] with fans as wings … a comic Kyōgen[40] danced by a homeless old man dressed as a little girl in Osaka … Yoshito Ohno[41] performing solo with a plastic red rose … a middle-aged Miyako Odori[42] dancer performing the character of 'Winter' in a simple dance play in Kyoto …

I know that experiences and events stand out in a luminous way when visiting a country for the first time – but I am objective enough to know when I am watching something sublime. Alongside the beauty and sophistication of both traditional and contemporary culture in Japan is the tragedy and legacy of its war experience. One of my most memorable experiences was visiting Hiroshima. The Memorial Peace Park is beautiful and serene with a constant flow of visitors paying their respects from all over Japan and abroad. The before-and-after images are terrible – but what one sees are people literally back on their bikes in a landscape of nothing. The strength the Japanese people demonstrated in the aftermath of the war, rebuilding their lives and their cities is very moving and extraordinary.

The fact that so much dance has survived through all of this is a reminder that it *is* very important. Everyone needs food, warmth, medicine, a roof, the basics – and we know that there are many people in the world who don't have those things. No one would deny that these basics should come first before art or dance; however it is interesting that art and dance very soon follow when there is any kind of infrastructure, as part of the survival process.

Personally dance has taken me on a journey towards becoming an artist and a teacher. I am interested in the lines of experience, and how those lines are expressed through the body as life information and as art. This usually means I prefer working with older dancers who have more lines … and I am looking forward to my own future as a dancer.

London 2010, developed from an earlier interview in August 1998.

Notes

1. The Place: home of London Contemporary Dance School, the London Contemporary Dance Theatre and later the Richard Alston Dance Company.
2. Strider (1972–75): dance company originally founded by Richard Alston, Jacky Lansley, Sally Potter, Di Davies, Dennis Greenwood, Christopher Banner and Wendy Levett. It has been called the UK's first postmodern dance company.
3. Richard Alston: UK choreographer, he was an early graduate of the London Contemporary Dance School, was a founder of Strider and later became Artistic Director of the Rambert Dance Company and then of The Place, including the Richard Alston Dance Company.
4. *Les Sylphides* (1909): choreographed for the Ballets Russes by Mikhail Fokine to music by Chopin, it was a distillation of the spirit of Romantic ballet.
5. Leonide Massine (1896 – 1979): brilliant character dancer and choreographer who first emerged with Diaghilev's Ballets Russes.
6. *La Boutique Fantasque*: a ballet conceived by Leonide Massine who wrote the choreography and the libretto. Originally made for Diaghilev's Ballets Russes in 1919, it was later remounted by the Royal Ballet.
7. Sally Potter: formed Limited Dance Company (1974–77) with Jacky Lansley, later joined by Rose English. Potter is a film director whose films include *The Gold Diggers, The London Story, Orlando, The Tango Lesson, The Man Who Cried, Yes* and *Rage*.
8. *Brief Encounter* (1974): a serial performance over three nights at Oval House Theatre, London, which explored and deconstructed archetypal imagery around trains, station platforms, arrivals and departures.
9. *Mounting* (1977): Structured improvised performance interacting with a Frank Stella exhibition at the Museum of Modern Art, Oxford, United Kingdom. Central themes were blood, memory, sharks (including those from *West Side Story*) show business, fear and politics. The performances were accompanied by a small book, *Mounting*, created by Potter, Lansley and English.
10. *Lochgilpead* (1974): Performed as part of the Richard Demarco Edinburgh Arts 74 programme in a small coastal town in Scotland. Lansley and Potter worked with a group of women students

to create a sequence of choreographed actions in the children's playground and surrounding landscape in coordination with the incoming tide.

11. Serpentine Gallery: art gallery situated in Kensington Gardens, London, which, for several years in the 1970s, ran a summer live art season in the gallery and its surrounding gardens.

12. X6 Collective: group of five dance artists – Emilyn Claid, Maedée Duprès, Fergus Early, Jacky Lansley and Mary Prestidge – who ran X6 Dance Space, a studio and performance space in the top floor of a warehouse in London's docklands – 1976–80. The collective also launched *New Dance* magazine in 1977, which for 11 years was a voice for new and experimental dance work in the United Kingdom.

13. *Dance Object* (1977): episodic solo with recorded voice exploring the subjective world of the performer's process. Choreographed, written and performed by Jacky Lansley.

14. Rose English: performance artist, writer and director who has been performing her own work for thirty years in venues such as Tate Britain, Royal Court Theatre, Queen Elizabeth Hall, the Adelaide Festival and Lincoln Center, New York. Her productions feature a diversity of co-performers including musicians, dancers, circus performers, magicians and horses.

15. The Women's Playhouse Trust: established in 1981 by Jules Wright, Diana Quick and Glenda Jackson with the aim of establishing a mainstream theatre in London where the work of women authors, directors, actors, producers and designers would be given centre stage.

16. Aphra Behn (1640–89): a prolific dramatist of the Restoration and one of the first English professional female writers.

17. The Royal Court: influential London theatre, at the forefront of new playwriting for more than 50 years.

18. Yuri Lyubimov: founder of the Taganka Theatre in Moscow, famous for its experimental productions, both before and after the fall of the Soviet regime.

19. Vsevolod Meyerhold: legendary Russian stage director and actor in the Soviet Union whose experimental work in the 1920s and 1930s led to the development of a physical training for actors known as biomechanics.

20. *The Breath of Kings* (1986): See contribution in *Body Space Image* by Miranda Tufnell and Chris Crickmay: Virago Press 1990.

21. Robert Helpmann (1909–86): Australian born actor, dancer and choreographer who performed with both The Old Vic Theatre and the Royal Ballet in a wide variety of principal roles.

22. *L'Autre*: Choreographer Jacky Lansley, music: from Igor Stravinsky's *Petrouchka*. Originally commissioned and produced by Christine Jowers as part of 'The Singular Voice of Woman' concert at The Place in 1997.

23. *Petrouchka* (1911): choreographed by Mikhail Fokine for the Ballets Russes and set in a nineteenth-century St Petersburg fairground, the main character is a puppet, originally played by Vaslav Nijinsky. Music by Igor Stravinsky.

24. Vaslav Nijinsky (1890–1951): principal dancer with Diaghilev's Ballets Russes and pioneering choreographer of works such as *L'Après-Midi d'un Faune* and *Rite of Spring*.

25. Mikhail Fokine (1880–1942): first great choreographer with the Ballets Russes, creating many enduring masterpieces.

26. *I, Giselle* (1980): a radical and seminal remake of the ballet *Giselle*, combining visual, dance and theatre disciplines. Drill Hall, London and United Kingdom tour. Choreographed and directed by Jacky Lansley and Fergus Early; music Stephen Montague after Adolphe Adam; designer Craig Givens; slide projections Jeanette Iljon; performers: Sue MacLennan, Suzy Gilmour, chris cheek [sic], Fergus Early, Jacky Lansley.

27. *Les Diables* (1998): a research project with actors and dancers at the University of North London (as part of Motion Pictures curated by director/writer Anna Furse) and Chisenhale Dance

which explored themes and images from Fokine and Stravinsky's ballet *The Firebird* resulting in a short documentary film *Through The Fire* by Jacky Lansley.

28. *Bird* (2001): a dance play drawing on material from Fokine and Stravinsky's ballet *The Firebird*, performed at the Southbank Centre, London and on tour. Written, choreographed and directed by Jacky Lansley. Performers included the actor Sonia Ritter as Bird and Fergus Early as The Employer.

29. *The Life Class* (2008): a short film transferring some of the themes and imagery from *Les Diables* and *Bird* to the world of corporate business. Cast also included actor dancer Tim Taylor (who worked with Lansley on *View from the Shore and Guests*) in the role of Kash.

30. Kathryn Pogson: English film, TV and stage actress. Her wide experience includes principal roles with the Royal Shakespeare Company and the feature film *Brazil*, as well as extensive work on TV. Also worked with Lansley on *The Lucky Chance* at the Royal Court.

31. Vincent Ebrahim: South African-born actor with extensive experience in a wide range of performance from community, experimental and mainstream theatre to successful TV comedy and drama. He also worked with Lansley on *Les Diables*, *Through The Fire* and a co-devised project *Small Dance*.

32. *Holding Space* (2004): choreographer Jacky Lansley; music: selected movements from Schubert's late piano sonatas – pianist Philip Gammon; Clore Studio, The Royal Opera House. Dancers: Sandra Conley, Tania Tempest-Hay, Lucy Tuck, Gareth Farley, Fergus Early and Robin Jung.

33. *View from the Shore* and *Anamule Dance* (2007): performed at Hall for Cornwall, Truro and the Clore Studio, London. *VFTS* music: Lindsay Cooper's *Concerto for Sopranino Saxophone and Strings* played live by the Cornish Sinfonia. *Anamule Dance* music: Jelly Roll Morton's 1930s recordings arranged and developed by composer Jonathan Eato.

34. *Standing Stones* (2009): made to Mozart's Clarinet Quintet (arrangement for piano and clarinet performed by members of The Cornish Sinfonia) for four dancers. Created for cathedral spaces including York Minster, Guildford, Wells and Exeter Cathedrals. Produced by Ascendance Rep.

35. *Guests*: an umbrella title for ongoing research which includes dialogues with Bach's unaccompanied Cello Suites and the Cornish landscape. In 2010, Lansley co-directed a cross art form research project with Tim Brinkman at the Hall for Cornwall as part of *Guests*.

36. Paul Burwell (1949–2007): UK percussionist influential in the fields of free improvisation and experimental art. Collaborators included David Toop and the sound-poet Bob Cobbing and in the 1980s he formed the Bow Gamelan Ensemble with Anne Bean and Richard Wilson.

37. Noh theatre: traditional Japanese theatre form, surviving almost unchanged from the thirteenth century. The text is in poetic form and is spoken, chanted and sung; dance and movement is an integral part of the form.

38. Nihon Buyo: traditional Japanese dance.

39. *The Dying Swan*: dance choreographed by Mikhail Fokine to music by Saint Saens and made famous all over the world by Russian ballerina Anna Pavlova (1881–1931).

40. Kyōgen: literally 'mad words' or 'wild speech' is a form of traditional Japanese comic theatre. It developed alongside Noh as an intermission between acts and retains close links to Noh in the modern day; therefore, it is sometimes designated noh-kyōgen.

41. Yoshito Ohno: see interview p. 73 and biography p. 192.

42. *Miyako Odori*: held every spring in the Gion district of Kyoto, Japan, the *Miyako Odori* is a season of performances of dance, centred on the annual cherry blossom festival, performed by newly graduated geishas ('Maiko') and their fully established older peers ('Geiko').

Chapter 8

Now We're Famous We Need Jackets

Will Gaines

Fergus: What started you dancing?

Will: I come from a town called Pontiac, Michigan, about 50 miles outside Detroit. I lived about 5 miles from the main road. It was all green grass and dirt roads. My father worked on the railroad, from Detroit to San Francisco and back. I just saw him on the weekends. Then he worked for General Motors, so when I was six, we moved to Detroit. The place looked good from the front, but inside, the roaches … ugh! You can't believe. Now I was in school and we were doing Snow White and the Seven Dwarves. I had a friend called Elmo – he couldn't walk straight, that's how out of tempo he was. He had no metre. Everybody else is white, but we two on the end are black, but we didn't know that, because we didn't think that way. I forget what characters we were, but we were the last two. So, that's the first time in show business! Later I go off to high school on the other side of town. I go to school with Tommy Flanagan, Kenny Burrel, Roland Hannah – all top jazz musicians. I actually went to school with these people. During the war, the teacher would lock us in the auditorium – the first class was English, which I should have woken up and gone to, but I was always late – the second class was a free hour in the auditorium, with a lovely grand piano, about 14 miles long, and we would have a jam session. Now, Tommy's brother played bass, somebody else played piano, and we would open this little door and all these instruments would fall out, all made out of brass or tin, painted brown – saxophones, trombones, everything, and we had a lovely piano. We would be locked in and we would jam. But the teacher would go out and go upstairs and sit in the balcony. Years later he told me that he locked us in because once we hit the streets, he knew we'd never come back! And he was right!

Now, a bit later, in 1948, I had a partner, and we'd been winning all the amateur shows – he had roller skates and I had tap dancing shoes, that was the novelty of the two of us. We'd perform in cinemas in the intermission between films, an amateur show of about four or five acts, and we would win two or five dollars. This lady booked us. She decided that we wasn't going to win any more – we'd been on the circuit long enough! We walked 9 miles from where we lived to a new town with a new cinema, built for war veterans coming home, and we won – we knew

Will Gaines dancing at the Greenwich Theatre, London, UK, in 1993.

we was going to win, so we didn't mind walking 9 miles – and the lady said, Great! And gives us a box of candy. We said, No, no – because we had no money to get back. We said, We'll take second prize, the two dollars, but she said, No, you won first prize. Now I realize that she was getting rid of us, because we were beating everybody, piano players, jugglers, comedians … So we couldn't sell this box of candy and we had to walk back home!

Later we did a show for Chryslers. It was a cold, cold winter, I'll never forget it. It was a night club – you've got to picture this lovely big supper club; there was a big big stage, for a big band, though in those days the musicians were staying home after the war, settling down, they hadn't really got back together. The dressing room was upstairs: you had everything you needed – a kitchen for cooking, an ironing board, you didn't have to go out for anything. I think the club held about 8–900 people. What we didn't know was that we were working with Louis Prima's[1] professional trio. The drummer was the leader – it was the first time I saw someone playing two bass drums – and he says, Where's your music? Well, I says, We just dance, you play it and we dance! So we go downtown to Broadway, Detroit, which is vaudeville houses and there's a music shop right in the middle and it's called Broadway music shop and in 1948 you got a pile of music about three inches high for a dollar. The tune we picked out was Perdido. Who is Duke Ellington? We don't know Duke Ellington! We got his music now, he wrote this tune! We took it back to the band – piano, bass, drums. So we worked out how much music we'd use and then we would have a finish. So he says, What's your finish? We say, Our finish is jumping over handkerchiefs. We're dancing in black trousers and white shirts, me in black tap dancing shoes and my partner in white skates. But now we're famous, we need jackets as well. So we had to go back downtown and buy two tail coats. Now we're back and our finish is jumping over handkerchiefs, the piano is going and the drummer is going, the bass player's loud, the piano player's loud, we're going to do flips, jump over our handkerchiefs and come off. And they're playing and we're dancing and it's going on and on and he says, What the f… are you doing?!! And I say, What we're doing is looking for our handkerchiefs that we put in our top pockets (because we'd bought conjurors' jackets and the handkerchiefs have disappeared down into a special compartment) and we is cussing, and the audience is laughing like hell, 'cos we is looking for our handkerchiefs! You don't stop and tell the bandleader you're looking for your handkerchief while they're playing, so when they realized what was going on they said, Finish for f…'s sake! So we do our flips and our splits, still trying to find our handkerchiefs, and stop!

Now I go to a night club called the Frolic Show Bar, and I win the amateur show, and the amateur show is paying 50 dollars a week, so I'm professional, and I'm on my own now. It's a bar in the daytime, one long bar but at night they put a stage down over the bar and in the well is the band – the saxophone player, the bass player, the trumpet player, the piano player and the drums. When you were on the stage you were not more than 3 feet from the ceiling, so if you jumped too high you would kill yourself. Now the compere was a man called Jo Jo Adams; he had tails, he was 10 foot tall, with a red chequer board suit; he was a comedian and blues singer from Chicago and because he was the star, he opened and closed the show. I was going on after him, so when he finished, he called me. He said, 'What's your name?' I says, 'Royce Edward Gaines'. So he says again, 'What's your name?' Because he couldn't hear me. I says again, 'Royce'. But he still couldn't hear me. So finally I shouted out 'Little Willie'. Well my mother used to say 'OK Little Willie', when I did something wrong, so I remembered Little Willie, you see. So Jo Jo Adams says 'Little Willie!' and on I go. Now the drummer's name was Babe Waters. He would play a rhythm and I was so bad, I would dance completely out of metre. But you didn't hear me, because he played so loud! We went on that way for 13 weeks with him playing behind me. During that time, somebody came into the club during the day and had an argument, and they shot a gun off. The bullet went through some glass at the side of the stage but didn't shatter it. So they put my picture over the bullet hole and people would ask, 'Who is that?' And they'd say, 'That's Little Willie. He's dancing'. So that's how I became famous!

Hymie, the club owner, found me an agent. So when I left the Frolic Show Bar, they sent me to another night club in the next state. When I got there, I said, 'I'm Little Willie'. They said, 'Yes, we've got your act'. I said, 'How come?' Well the drummer had called the next night club (in those days all the musicians knew each other) and told him how bad I was and what I couldn't do! And then when I went on to Dayton, Ohio, he called that drummer and that drummer would call the next one … this went on for almost 2 years. Then eventually the comperes picked me up – a compere would take me with him on his show, so when he got to a town, he would have two acts, himself and me, so he could make up the show from anyone in town.

So I learnt to tap dance by listening to the musicians. When I learnt the melody, the little phrases the saxophone player or the piano player was playing, I had another step. I put these steps together without knowing how to do it, but I did it.

Fergus: Just going right back to the time you were jamming in high school, how did you get the ideas for what you were doing? Did you see people tapping in the movies?

Will: Oh yes, we saw the movies, we saw Donald O'Connor,[2] we saw Fred Astaire[3] and in all the little short black movies that were made, you had tap dancers in them – mostly gangster movies, set in Harlem. But when I was still at school, we used to go and watch a dancer called Teddy Hale at a theatre called the Paradise – Aretha Franklin's[4] father bought it for her – that was the vaudeville house. I saw everybody there – Count Basie,[5] Duke Ellington,[6] Fatha Hines,[7] Billy Eckstine[8] when he was a roadie, Sarah Vaughan[9] when she was the relief piano player for Fatha Hines – many of today's famous musicians when they were just starting. I didn't know who I was looking at, at the time. So we used to go to the Paradise and see these dancers.

Patterson and Jackson was two lads out of Detroit, they sang and they danced. They was each of them about ten tons, but to see them dance, it was like dancing on a feather, you wouldn't believe they could be looking that light when they were moving their feet. So I was watching Teddy Hale, Honi Coles and Chuck Green, Baby Lawrence, Snappy White and Red Fox[10]– all these people and I learned from them, but the musicians playing for me had to keep me in time.

Jacky: You invented your own steps?

Will: No, I'm afraid they'd already been invented by Charlie Parker, Dizzie Gillespie, Bud Powell[11] and I just hummed them! People used to ask me 'Why don't you lift your feet up?', you know, like the buck dancing and kicking and jumping over your foot. I used to say, 'They don't pay enough money up there, so I keep my feet on the ground!'

Chris Parry: (Will's manager and a dancer herself): But, originally, most of his steps come from the clog dance. It's different rhythms and phrasing but you dance with the whole foot. At first in America they were picking their feet up, bucking and winging and all that, and then when they started to dance jazz, it became very floory. Also, he's not thinking arms and show business presentation, he's thinking rhythms and sounds.

Jacky: So you've worked with all the great jazz musicians and singers?

Will: Oh yes. For example, I knew Eartha Kitt[12] before she had a change of knickers! She went to Toronto and they just didn't want to know about her. The disc jockey in the club downstairs used to let her sleep in his room – she didn't have enough money to get a place. Then all of a sudden George Shearing picked up on her; a lot of people don't know that George Shearing produced a lot of artists.

Then she was a star. So when we got to New York we were playing the Apollo and I was the newest thing with the Cotton Club show at the same time. I was with Martha Raye,[13] Jimmy Durante[14] and all the big acts. This was 1959 and I had a '59 Buick. After we finish at the Apollo, I'm playing the Concord in the Catskill Mountains, with Eartha Kitt again, and I have to carry her to the Catskills from New York in my brand new Buick. But when I wake up in the morning they'd taken my car away, because I ain't paid the payments! I knew I'd got to take Eartha Kitt, so I had to go out and buy an old car. Guess what I bought? An old 1950 Chrysler! I can't remember where I got the money to buy it – it must have cost about 80 dollars! You can imagine what it looked like when I turn up on Broadway to pick up Eartha Kitt. Naturally she thought I was taking the mickey … I don't know who brought her back, but it wasn't me!

Chris: She went through an awful lot in her life. She was mixed race …

Will: And she came from down South where they mistreated her as well.

Chris: The racism then was horrendous.

Will: But she was a dancer (did you know that?) and so she knows how to go up and down.

Jacky: So when did you come over here?

Will: In 1963. When I came to England, I was just getting my act together to do jazz – I'd done the Cotton Club and I'd done the overseas shows for American bases and I wanted to do proper jazz, none of this doing the same show every night, 8 minutes, taking a bow and all that crap! But what happened was that William Morris, my agents, sent me a telegram to go to England, to the Pigalle, with Shani Wallis. Later I found out it was Sammy Davis Junior[15] who recommended me. I'd worked with Sammy many years before that in Buffalo. We did shows for the hospital, for the veterans who'd come back from the Korean war. And now he was over here in England with Norman Miller and we'd all been together at the Cotton Club. Now the dancer that was over here was Teddy Hale and he was a master tap dancer who I'd watched as I came up, but he'd been giving everybody a problem at the Pigalle and the Palladium, so Al Burnett said to Sammy Davis, 'Do you know a clean tap dancer?' – meaning one who wasn't an alcoholic or a dope addict, so Sammy recommended me, because he knew that I copied Teddy Hale: I kept my feet close to the floor and did riffs, like you were listening to a drummer.

One time, I was working the Pigalle and after the show I'm walking down by the Talk of the Town, in Leicester Square, and I hear this voice saying, 'Come over here Willie' and it's one of the buskers who are dancing in the streets. He has this little record player playing Oscar Peterson[16] and he's dancing away and I says, 'OK, I'll try that tonight!' These buskers said they went over to do the Ed Sullivan show[17] every year, but then they told Ed Sullivan to piss off because they were making more money busking in London than doing his show in New York!

Now they put me on Sunday Night at the Palladium,[18] with Tommy Cooper,[19] Shirley Bassey and Norman Vaughan[20] as the new compere and the Jack Parnell Orchestra.[21] Don't tell me that white folks don't have rhythm, because that orchestra had rhythm! Anyhow, I did the show and they asked me to do the television show, which I did. And then I thought I was out of there and back to Germany to do the shows for the troops. But then I got a call to be back at the Palladium within two weeks, which I was! From then on, I did nine Sunday Nights at the Palladium. I worked with all the stars – Mike and Bernie Winters,[22] Humperdinck,[23] Dave Allen,[24] Morecambe and Wise,[25] but I hardly knew who they were, because every time I'd do a show I'd have to go out of the country, because I was only allowed 6 months at a time.

Then I started to go to Greaseborough Working Men's Club in Doncaster – that was the big working man's club at the time. And I started going to other clubs in Manchester and so on and the next thing I knew I'd been here 5 years and got residency. And then I finally got back into jazz. I was living in Rotherham and one night Alex Welsh[26] came through, picked me up and took me to the Queen Elizabeth Hall and then Humphrey Lyttelton[27] at the Festival Hall. I was back into jazz, and I wasn't going back to no more night clubs! And that's where I'm at now.

Will Gaines dancing in Scarborough, UK, in 1968.

Fergus: Nowadays, do you always dance with the same band?

Chris: When we turn up for a gig, quite often we don't even know the musicians. We've booked them and we may have our own MD, but nothing is rehearsed. So Will is a jazz musician first and he improvises all evening. He doesn't know what they're going to play, he doesn't know the arrangements, he doesn't know anything. I find that remarkable.

Fergus: But you do work some of the time with the same bands?

Will: With some of the same musicians. For example, I've been working with Stan Tracey, with the orchestra, doing Duke Ellington's Sacred Concert. I did it originally with Duke in Cambridge, when he came over. I was working in a club in Malmo, Sweden, and Duke was giving a concert at the concert hall. I said to Herbie Jones,[28] who was arranging all my music, 'Is the maestro going to do the Sacred Concert when he gets to England?' When I came down in the hotel next morning, there was a telegram on the desk saying, 'Be at the Palladium at 8 o'clock in the morning.' So I packed my bags, jumped on the airplane and landed in England. When we were rehearsing for the show in Cambridge, Duke is sitting there, and Rufus Jones the drummer, and Duke says 'Willie, what's your tempo?' I said, 'Well, I've heard the record …' it was Bunny Briggs[29] and Louis Nelson[30] doing that bit – just drums and feet '… I've heard Bunny Briggs …' and Duke says again 'Willie, again what's your tempo?' I said, 'Maestro, I've heard …' and he says 'Willie, WHAT'S YOUR TEMPO?' And I said, 'As a matter of fact, maestro, it's just a bit faster!' So I go over to Rufus Jones and I said, 'If you hum How High the Moon, that's what I'll be humming', even though the orchestra would be playing something quite else!

Jacky: Do you wear taps on toes and heels?

Will: Yes. Capezio's[31] I used to have some with a left foot tap and a right foot tap. They don't make them any more, but they had a sound … Bunny Briggs, he was the one give them to me, at the Apollo.

Fergus: Do you wear them quite loose?

Will: If I can. They're new now, so they're loud – I hate it when they're loud.

(Will plays us a sound recording of a performance he gave in Holland. He is introduced by Derek Bailey,[32] the doyen of English 'free' music, and then gives an amazing unaccompanied solo for around 7 minutes. What is remarkable is not only the rhythmic complexity and felicity, but also, revealed here by the lack of instrumental playing, the magical range and dynamic of the sound itself, painting a truly musical picture through the air waves.)

Chris: If you're any sort of dancer or musician, you can hear the cross-rhythms he does, but if you compare that to most drummers, how often do you hear a drummer that can make it as interesting as that?

Will: And the drummer's got more things to make different sounds, I've just got that floor and I can't dampen it.

Fergus: Do you ever work on more than one surface?

Will: Yes. I carry a board around with me.

Fergus: When you're dancing unaccompanied, do you always keep tunes going in your head, like when you told Rufus Jones to hum How High the Moon?

Will: No, I don't any longer. I used to, but now I've learnt to just keep the steps and phrases in my head.

Fergus: I found I was listening to the tape like a story.

Will: That's what an old-timer said to me, he said, 'Paint that story when you're out there with an audience, paint that story.'

Chris: That's why to me, he's a musician first, then he's a dancer.

Will: That's where I come from, musicians. But now, in this country, I often have musicians who want to come in on me. They want to play. So I leave them out for 20 minutes, because the minute they sit down behind me, they want to come in, they don't want to sit there! When I saw Teddy Hale dance Begin the Beguine and he cut the musicians out, those were musicians who knew what he was doing – to me, he was actually dancing the melody. When I got here, the musicians were used to doing a routine, so then I had to stop doing an act, and I started doing my own 2-hour show. Of course I have worked with great musicians here, like Stan Tracey,[33] who's up there with Thelonius Monk[34] and Duke Ellington.

Fergus: Do you do anything to keep fit, other than perform?

Will: I got a shed. Many years ago, when I grew up, the tap dancers would go in their garage or their basement and just dance – people like Honi Coles, Chuck Green – and they'd come out with a routine and the musicians would put the music to it. Now, I got a shed, and a lot of wood, and I'm going to lay that down. Then I'm going to set up my two cameras, one on my feet, and record what happens. I'm going to make a video book for future tap dancers.

Leigh on Sea, UK, 1 June 2000

Shortly after this interview we went to see Will dance in a pub in Leytonstone, East London, as part of a local jazz festival. He was supported by three jazz musicians and he'd told us beforehand to bring our tap shoes along as there'd be an opportunity to join in. Will's act was much as it had been 20 years earlier, with no concessions to his age (he was now in his early 70s). The music played, Will danced. Sometimes the music stopped and Will continued to dance. Sometimes he talked as he danced – a continuous stream of jokes that reeled out, as seamlessly as the sound that emanated from the four plates of metal at his toes and heels.

The moment came for joining in – 'sitting in' as a jazz musician would put it. We hesitated. Fortunately. Four people got up, obviously ready and eager, doing up their tap shoes. Soon they were jamming with Will, all of a high technical standard and differing styles, though none with quite Will's nonchalant ease. All, though, were way above anything we, with our long distant ISTD tap exams, could hope to emulate. We sat tight. It turned out they were all professionals, dancing in various shows, who'd turned up to dance with this extraordinary man wearing his reversed baseball cap and T – shirt (as he'd done decades before it was ever thought fashionable here) and who'd danced with many of the greatest jazz musicians of the century, on the stages of Harlem's Apollo and London's Palladium and many a pub, arts centre and working man's club the length of Britain. This was not a glamorous gig. Maybe 60 people watched, but Will's commitment was total and commanded our rapt attention.

Notes

1. Louis Prima (1910–78): a Sicilian-American singer, actor, songwriter and trumpeter. Prima rode the musical trends of his time, starting with his seven-piece New Orleans style jazz band in the 1920s, then successively leading a swing combo in the 1930s, a big band in the 1940s, a Vegas lounge act in the 1950s and a pop-rock band in the 1960s.
2. Donald O'Connor (1925–2003): US tap dancer, actor, appeared in many Hollywood movies with Gene Kelly, Fred Astaire, etc.
3. Fred Astaire (1899–1987): US actor, singer and probably the greatest film tap dancer of the twentieth century.
4. Aretha Franklin : US singer, perhaps the foremost proponent of the genre known as 'soul', she has been called the 'Queen of Soul'.
5. Count Basie (1904–84): US pianist and bandleader, a leading figure of the swing era of jazz.
6. Edward Kennedy 'Duke' Ellington (1899–1974): pianist, bandleader and probably the greatest jazz composer of the twentieth century.
7. Earl 'Fatha' Hines (1903–83): brilliant US jazz pianist, at the forefront of jazz development from the 1920s to the 1970s. Downbeat Magazine elected him 'No 1 Jazz Pianist' six times in the 1960s and 1970s.
8. Billy Eckstine (1914–93): American singer of ballads and bandleader of the swing era. Eckstine's smooth baritone and distinctive vibrato broke down barriers throughout the 1940s, first as leader of the original bop big-band, then as the first romantic black male in popular music.
9. Sarah Vaughan (1924–90): US jazz singer, described by Scott Yanow as having one of the most wondrous voices of the 20th century. The National Endowment for the Arts bestowed upon her its 'highest honor in jazz', the NEA Jazz Masters Award, in 1989.
10. Teddy Hale, Honi Coles, Chuck Green, Baby Lawrence, Snappy White, Red Fox, all distinguished US jazz tap dancers.
11. Charlie Parker (1920–55) saxophone player, Dizzie Gillespie (1917–93) trumpeter, Bud Powell (1924–66) pianist, three of the most influential post-war generation of bebop jazz musicians.
12. Eartha Kitt (1927–2008): US actress, singer and cabaret star. She was perhaps best known for her highly distinctive singing style.
13. Martha Raye (1916–94): US comic actress and standards singer who performed in movies, and later on television.
14. Jimmy Durante (1893–1980): US singer, pianist, comedian and actor – vaudeville, film and TV performer.
15. Sammy Davis Junior (1925–90): US singer, tap dancer, actor, one of the famous 'rat pack' with Frank Sinatra, Dean Martin, etc.
16. Oscar Peterson (1925–2007): Canadian jazz pianist and composer. He released over 200 recordings, won seven Grammy Awards, and received other numerous awards and honours

over the course of his career. He is considered to have been one of the finest jazz pianists of all time.

17. Ed Sullivan show: variety show on US TV which carried great kudos for those who appeared on it in the 1950s and 1960s.

18. Sunday Night at the London Palladium: variety show broadcast on UK TV every Sunday night for much of the 1950s and 1960s.

19. Tommy Cooper (1921–84): UK comedian, famous for his magic tricks that didn't work.

20. Norman Vaughan (1923–2002): UK TV and stage presenter and compere.

21. Jack Parnell Orchestra: UK big band led by drummer Jack Parnell.

22. Mike and Bernie Winters: UK comedian double act, originally in music hall, later on TV.

23. Englebert Humperdinck: popular UK singer of 1960s, 1970s and 1980s.

24. Dave Allen (1936–2005): Irish comedian who became very popular on UK TV.

25. Eric Morecambe (1926–84) and Ernie Wise (1925–1999): UK comedy double act, originally in music hall and later the most popular comics on UK TV.

26. Alex Welsh (1929–82): a Scottish jazz musician, who played the cornet, trumpet and sang.

27. Humphrey Lyttelton (1921–2008): also known as Humph, leading UK jazz musician, also popular presenter of radio shows.

28. Herbie Jones (1926–2001): US jazz trumpeter, music composer and arranger.

29. Bunny Briggs: prominent US tap dancer who was inducted into the American Tap Dancing Hall of Fame in 2006.

30. Louis Nelson: US jazz drummer.

31. Capezio: US dancewear manufacturer.

32. Derek Bailey (1930–2005): English avant-garde guitarist and leading figure in the free improvisation movement.

33. Stan Tracey: prominent UK jazz pianist, composer and bandleader.

34. Thelonious Monk (1917–82): jazz pianist and composer considered one of the giants of American music.

Chapter 9

That Quality of Knowing Movement Never Leaves You

Jane Dudley

Jane Dudley in her piece *Harmonica Breakdown*, 1937. Photograph: © Barbara Morgan, The Barbara Morgan Archive

The first section of this interview was conducted as part of the research for 'Tales from the Citadel', in 1996, in which Jane subsequently performed. Jane had recently had a second hip replacement operation and, following that, a knee operation, and was just starting rehearsing for the show, while at the same time recuperating from the surgery.

Fergus: What was your early training?

Jane: In 1931, I had been down at North Carolina in rather an unusual college at Chapel Hill University; I was there for 3 months. After 3 months, I said to myself: If I want to dance, this isn't an environment that's going to be useful for me. So I came back to New York, and went into the Wigman School[1] in January. I was one of the youngest of the pupils, I think I was barely 18 and I worked like stink. It gave me a tremendous lift, you know.

Fergus: Were you working every day?

Jane: Yes. Hanya [Holm][2] had a real school. We started with technique in the morning. We had improvisation – group improvisation, which she directed. We had percussion. We had a dance evening once a month, where we showed what we'd done. We started at 9 in the morning and we didn't get done till about 4. It was a very good solution for me, because it meant my day was structured and I wasn't left to my own devices, which I think is very hard for a young 17-, 18-, 19-year old.

I stayed with Hanya Holm for 4 years. I have certain reservations about the method, but I'm very glad I did it, because when I started to teach and began what I called the movement class, things that I'd done with Hanya came back to me. And, as far as I know, improvisation was an unknown word at that time, and it was really the German school that brought it over. The structure of the class was very interesting and depended on a very good teacher. The class worked in space all the time. You started in a circle, very often, and then you went across the floor on the diagonal, so every single technical thing you did was on the diagonal. There would be a theme for a class, which might, for example, be hip movement. So everything – the walk used the hip in a special way, the leg was swung in a special way, you leaped in a special way, mainly around circles and curves in space, because they came out of the use of the hip. And that was unique to the Wigman work. Swing, that was unique, and vibration, where you kept a steady pulse in the heel …

Fergus: It's interesting, Tim [Rubidge][3] was showing us some Laban swing scales today, and Laban worked a lot with Wigman, they experimented a lot together and I was interested in that relationship.

Jane: He was her teacher, of course. I don't think we ever did with Hanya the full scale of swings, she wasn't into that sort of thing. But I remember when I used vibrations[4] in the movement class I taught at the London School of Contemporary Dance, the kids went berserk, because it's very intoxicating. It's very primitive. I used to have one of our good percussionists play for the class. So, all of that – swing, vibration, *passivity* … For example you can't do curves without a certain *letting* – you have to feel the centre of gravity. You can't do it with your will, your body has to yield to it – it's a very valuable experience. Then there's the opposite, the active scale, where you're directing everything – sharp changes of direction use the active scale, for example. There can be a passive leap or an active leap. Stamping was an active walk, a passive walk was a gliding walk. When I was teaching movement classes, it was so hard to get across: the students couldn't let their backs give to the curve and *create* the curve.

So, as I said, I'm very glad I had that experience. But all the time I wanted to go to work with Martha [Graham]. So finally, Bennington Summer School[5] was started. That was in 1934. The first 6-week course at Bennington in beautiful Vermont was held in 1935. All the outstanding figures in modern dance – Martha, Doris [Humphrey],[6] Charles [Weidmann][7] and Hanya – had courses going on at the same time. Martha's was the first workshop and I think there were 35 of us chosen to be in her workshop: that's quite a mob! She asked if I would be a member of her company at the end of that summer. I remember being so intoxicated by her classes that I felt about 2 inches above the ground. When I was talking to a journalist from the BBC this morning, he said something about dancing when you're so old. I said, well you know, it's an interesting thing: there's something you never lose – your body may not respond to what is inside your head, but that quality of knowing movement never leaves you. And I can tell you something else: it also is your eye when you see other people dance – you know whether they're real dancers or whether they've just *learned*.

I was very much involved in the left. I think we all were, because it was the time of the depression. So social content was something we were all working with and trying to find approaches to. Now some of it was very naïve and really agitprop and pretty silly! But at least it gave us a focus and it gave us an audience. And that was the most wonderful thing, because it was audiences who were all wanting to see and hear what we were doing. I've never forgotten that and it also gave one a tremendous impetus to compose, because you felt you were doing it for a cause, a purpose, for *people*. You weren't just doing it for yourself.

Fergus: Martha, though, wouldn't have been involved in that overtly political scene, would she?

Jane: No. Martha stayed separate. That was part of her genius, to stay separate. But, what was interesting was that she was very much influenced by what was happening in the social scene and also, because of the way she was dancing, she felt herself very much a heretic, an outsider, not accepted by the public.

And she did dances like *Steerage and Strike*, *The Horses of the Apocalypse*, *Heretic*. Now *Heretic* was the individual against the stereotype mob – the do-gooders versus the fragile, rebellious alien figure. Those feelings really fertilized her for quite a long while. Doris [Humphrey] was doing American sorts of things. That was one of the things they were all concerned with, finding an American style.

Fergus: I suppose Martha did too, with things like *Appalachian Spring*.

Jane: Yes. *Appalachian Spring* was a later work, but in those early days she did dances like *American Provincials*. And the other thing of course that was strong in Martha was the conflict between the spirit and the flesh – Puritanism and hedonism.

Anyhow, I joined Martha's company, but a group of six of us decided to start a new professional revolutionary group called the New Dance Group. We got someone from Martha's company, Sophie Maslow,[8] to come and teach us. We got Mr [Louis] Horst[9] to come and teach us composition, we got somebody from the Group Theatre,[10] which was at that time working very strongly with the Stanislavsky method, to come and talk about it and we had classes every morning and rehearsals. We weren't ready for it, of course. I told Martha I thought it might interfere with her work. She was absolutely furious. The other dancers in the New Dance Group whom I'd sacrificed my career for didn't seem to care. So, I began to regret it more and more and more and more and that summer I went up to Bennington with my mother and I asked Martha if she would take me back. She said she would. Well, I'm telling you … on her terms! I didn't get a part, I sat out of rehearsals; and it really wasn't until '38 that I got anything to do, when she did *American Document*, which was a revolutionary piece, in its way. It was based on the important documents that made American history: the Declaration of Independence, Lincoln's speech at Gettysburg. Then there was the wonderful duet she did with Erick Hawkins,[11] when he first joined the company. The dance was accompanied by spoken sections of the Song of Songs, alternating with passages from the sermons of Jonathan Edwards.

Of course we couldn't bear it, because Martha immediately fell head over heels in love with Erick and we all were jealous, particularly as Martha asked him to rehearse us and that was the final insult. When we were rehearsing *American Document*, he said, 'Well now, your arms are all different. I think you should do it the way Ethel[12] does it.' Well now, we were all furious at that as we always felt our arms should go where our backs told them to go. I think he lasted about two rehearsals and then poor Sophie had to do the rest of it.

Fergus: Erick Hawkins was ballet trained?

Jane: Yes. He was a classmate with Leo[13] and a Greek scholar, a Greek major. I don't know what on earth made him go into ballet. He was tall and beautifully built – he was really a stunning looking man. He went into Lincoln Kirsten's[14] first attempt to start a ballet company, Ballet Caravan.[15]

Fergus: Pre Balanchine?[16]

Jane: Yes, Balanchine had not come over yet. At any rate, as I said, Martha fell head over heels in love with him. Louis couldn't stand him, of course, and it began to get worse and worse. But Erick was good for Martha. First of all he was tall and stunning to look at, and she was small, you see. And also, then he began to get music commissions for her and he got her to use some kind of decor – I think that was when Noguchi[17] started to work with her. And then men came into the company, and that made a big difference, too.

Fergus: No men before that?

Jane: No. It was all women. Twelve women.

Fergus: That must have been a major change, then, in dynamic.

Jane: Yes. It completely changed the nature of the dances. Because before that, we were really not characters, we were a chorus. That was how Martha used us. Sometimes with us as her backdrop. Sometimes we danced without her.

So, I consider those years with Martha the most important formative years of my life. I worked very seriously on her pieces and it trained me how to work seriously on my own. We learned to do a certain amount of reading background so we informed ourselves about her dances, when we did Emily Dickinson, for example, or the Bronte's, and when I did my own dances later, I did a lot of background reading.

Fergus: How do you keep fit, nowadays? I know you're in a recovery situation at the moment, so it's rather a special time.

Jane: Well, what I was doing in recent times was a series of exercises mostly on the floor. I did a few standing swings, I think, which I realized about 3 years ago were very hard. I lost my balance, just doing a forward and back swing. I worked with Joseph Pilates[18] in New York when I had a bad hip. Now, it's a question of doing my own exercises and really mainly strengthening my legs and my arms and my back and my stomach muscles. I'm about to start with some body conditioning work with Alan Herdman[19] and I'll see. I don't want to have a crutch. If I have a cane, all right. I was walking with a cane before. I don't know if I'll ever be able to walk completely freely.

It's interesting, I did two pieces in the last few years which I did really out of my head. I just used very good dancers that I could direct, and occasionally I'd show what I wanted, if I wasn't getting it across. They were reconstructions of early dances. One was to a poem and one was a trio.

Fergus: Were you just remembering, or were you re-inventing?

Jane: No. In each case I remembered the end. I remembered the end of *Short Story* and it had a story, so I could hang the movement on that. *Time is Money* was a very radical poem, a red-hot radical poem that I had done in '34, and I remembered one phrase of movement and the rest was all reconstructed. But the thing that's interesting is that because you've lived much, much longer, you have many more resources to draw from and that's what I felt was a godsend in the case of both dances. And not only resources – you have experiences that you draw from and that makes it that much richer. That's one reason why, as an older dancer, you have something you can contribute, just because of your long experience and the things that you know, that you've been through.

Fergus: And mostly we're denied that experience, because so few people get to be older dancers.

London, 4 September 1996

The second part of the interview that follows was recorded in 1999. In the intervening years, Jane had continued to choreograph and perform into her late 80s.

Fergus: We wanted to talk a little more about your current performing. When you are performing, I'm very conscious of the sheer power of your presence.

Jane: I think the quality of performance is something one has, unconsciously, inside. And then I think it's a question of feeding it when you are on stage. Certain roles require it. The role I had to play in *Letter to the World*, which was the dance Martha did based on Emily Dickinson,[20] and where the movement that she gave me was pretty spare – if I didn't use all the power that was within me, it would have been very unconvincing, I'm quite sure.

Jacky: From the wonderful experience I had dancing with you in *Tales from the Citadel*[21] I certainly sensed a great power emanating from you, so what you're describing there, in that Emily Dickinson piece was that you'd learnt to work with the minimal.

Jane: Yes. But you have to have something with substance to it, to work with, which I did have as the Isadora Duncan[22] character, Aura, in *Tales from the Citadel*. Duncan must have had that to an extraordinary degree.

Jacky: Did you enjoy overlapping with Duncan and thinking about her and working with her character?

Jane: Yes, I did. I always identified with her. It was very funny. When I went to camp as a 12-year old, and I'd just read *My Life in Dance*,[23] I made a soft wool, raspberry tunic for myself, long to my ankles, and I wore sandals, à la Duncan!

Jacky: You're such an expressive performer, you're an actress-dancer.

Jane: Yes, I think that is true. I will accept that. I think that developed. Just after I left Martha's company, someone said to me: 'Have you ever thought of being an actress?' But I hadn't. I don't think I would have dared take on that responsibility,

Jane Dudley quoting Isadora Duncan's 'La Marseillaise', with Brian Bertscher in *Tales from the Citadel*, 1996 by Green Candle Dance Company. Photograph: Dee Conway

because I was close to the Group Theatre at that time and I realized what a terrific responsibility they carried, in order to make something come alive. I was too conscious that you couldn't just play around with acting. One of the things we were all deeply trained not to allow to happen was what you'd call 'indicating' – doing the outside instead of working from the process inside you. I was influenced by all this much more than anyone else in Martha's company, I think.

Jacky: Was Martha influenced by Stanislavski?[24]

Jane: She was. There's a very nice article in Ballet Review,[25] in which Dorothy Bird[26] talks about her first experience with Martha. The images that Martha gave her to work with were very much acting ones. I always felt that Dorothy was the best of Martha's dancers. She talked about using a horse as an image, and how she champed at the bit. Of course some of the urges in those beginning years, with the prancing and so forth, were very animal-like. I was surprised at how concrete the images were that Dorothy used. I also was interested that Martha had come upon this way of working. You didn't see that consciously in her work, but Martha used very concrete images sometimes. Once she said that when she danced *American Provincials* and she came out to do the solo, she stood behind the centre split in the curtains and she said to God 'I'm here God.' And then she came on centre stage. I always thought that was a wonderful impetus, a wonderful thing around which to build the power of an entrance. And it certainly was – she came walking on with all the drive of a prophet.

That was one reason why she got so much out of the Neighbourhood Playhouse[27] students, because she did approach them from an acting point of view, all the time. I remember her coming in to the centre of the back of the Playhouse dance studio and standing for a moment. Then she strode down, the way she would, and she said 'The trouble with that movement is there's no *Kundalini*'. Now I don't think the kids knew what *Kundalini* was from a hole in the wall ... I certainly didn't! But it was later explained to me that it was the cobra or the black snake that rested at the base of the spine and when it was awakened it uncoiled and came up the back to the base of the neck and then the dancer becomes alive. You know Agnes[28] has a short chapter on Kundalini in her book on Martha.

Jacky: Do you think your actorly and expressive skills have sustained you as a performer into your older age?

Jane: Yes, I do. If you are working in a form of dance that allows that to be used, that is another richness that you can bring to your work.

Fergus: How was it making the material for the film *Dancing Inside*?[29]

Jane: It was interesting. What I did was to work entirely from the music. With the Webern (*for which Jane made herself a solo performed mainly with hands and face*), there was a little bit of a religious atmosphere in it. I felt a bit as though I were using the 'teaching hand' that Christ might have used, or one of the disciples might have used. I didn't try to make it a religious dance; I just felt that I could believe in it better that way.

Jane Dudley with Tim Rubidge in *Tales from the Citadel*, 1996, by Green Candle Dance Company. Photograph: Hugo Glendinning

Jacky: In your performance now, you're certainly getting across what you want to express. Do you find it very effortful? Is it a pleasure for you, your recent performance work?

Jane: Yes. Yes. It has been, up to a point. Hard work, but there must be a lot of narcissism to it, you know. The feeling you're being looked at, and so forth. You see, most of what I've had to do recently has been fairly restrained. It hasn't caused me to get out of breath (although I think there was one part in Citadel where I did get out of breath), but generally, I didn't, and that of course was a help. That's the limitations of my heart. So I'm going to go back to work with Alan [Herdman] to see how much I can regenerate in me. The body is certainly a very mysterious thing.

London, UK, 23 July 1999

Jane Dudley died in September 2001 at the age of 89.

Notes

1. The Wigman School: founded in New York by the great German modern dancer, Mary Wigman, and run by one of her most distinguished pupils, Hanya Holm.
2. Hanya Holm (1893–1992): born and trained in Germany, she went to New York to run the Wigman School. She is known as one of the 'Big Four' founders of American modern dance, along with Martha Graham, Charles Wiedman and Doris Humphrey. She was a dancer, choreographer and, above all, a dance educator.
3. Tim Rubidge: dancer, teacher and choreographer who lives in Northumberland, United Kingdom; much of his work has been site-specific and with rural communities. He also works widely in the sphere of arts and health, often collaborating with the dance practitioner Miranda Tufnell.
4. Vibrations: a movement in the Wigman technique where the standing leg pulses with a softened knee and a bounce in the heel.
5. Bennington Summer School: a summer programme, known as the Bennington School of Dance, run in the 1930s and attracting many people, among them Martha Graham, Martha Hill and José Limón.
6. Doris Humphrey (1895–1958): pioneering US dancer and choreographer, author of *The Art of Making Dances*.
7. Charles Weidman (1901–75): choreographer, modern dancer and teacher, well known as one of the pioneers of modern dance in America. Much of his work was with Doris Humphrey.
8. Sophie Maslow (1911–2006): American choreographer, dancer and teacher and founding member of New Dance Group. She became a member of Martha Graham's Company in 1931, performing many solo roles, until 1943. She created her own dance troupe, The Sophie Maslow Dance Company and, with Jane Dudley and William Bales, established the Dudley-Maslow-Bales Trio in 1942.
9. Louis Horst (1884–1964): composer and musical adviser for the Martha Graham Company for many years, he was one of the first people ever to teach choreography as a distinct discipline.
10. Group Theatre (1931–41): New York City theatre collective formed by Harold Clurman, Cheryl Crawford and Lee Strasberg. They were pioneers of what would become an 'American acting

technique' derived from the teachings of Konstantin Stanislavski, but pushed beyond them as well. The company included actors, directors, playwrights and producers.

11. Erick Hawkins (1909–94): leading US modern dance choreographer and dancer. He was the first man to dance with Martha Graham's company and was later married to her for some years. He formed his own company and worked to redefine dance technique according to the principles of kinesiology.

12. Ethel Butler (1914–96): long-standing principal dancer with Martha Graham and later respected teacher.

13. Leo Hurwitz (1909–91): Jane Dudley's former and late husband; he was an award-winning documentary film maker who dealt with social justice and similar themes.

14. Lincoln Edward Kirstein (1907–96): American writer, impresario, art connoisseur and cultural figure in New York City. Together with Edward M. M. Warburg and the Russian choreographer George Balanchine, he founded the American Ballet, later to become New York City Ballet.

15. Ballet Caravan (1936–41): founded by Kirstein to produce works by young American choreographers, presented many American ballet dancers in the early works of Eugene Loring, Lew Christensen, and William Dollar.

16. George Balanchine (1904–83): Russian Dancer and choreographer who made his first work for Diaghilev's Ballets Russes and later founded New York City Ballet with Lincoln Kirstein.

17. Noguchi: Isamu Noguchi (1904–88): prominent Japanese American artist and landscape architect whose career spanned six decades, from the 1920s onward. Known for his sculpture and public works, Noguchi designed stage sets for various Martha Graham productions.

18. Joseph Hubertus Pilates (1883–1967): invented the Pilates method of physical fitness which focuses attention on core postural muscles that help keep the human body balanced and provide support for the spine.

19. Alan Herdman: founder of the Body Conditioning Studio, using weight-based exercise for conditioning and recovery, based on the work of Joseph Pilates.

20. Emily Dickinson (1830–86): US poet, fewer than a dozen of whose 1800 poems were published during her lifetime. Dickinson's poems are unique for the era in which she wrote; many of them deal with themes of death and immortality and use unconventional syntax.

21. *Tales from the Citadel*: see Introduction p. 11.

22. Isadora Duncan (1877–1927): US dancer, considered by many to be the creator of modern dance. She rejected traditional ballet steps to stress improvisation, emotion and the human form. She became so famous that she inspired artists and authors to create sculpture, jewellery, poetry, novels, photographs, watercolours, prints and paintings of her.

23. *My Life in Dance:* Isadora Duncan's autobiography.

24. Stanislavski (1863–1938): Russian theatre director and theoretician whose practice and writing were enormously influential. His ideas were taken up in the United States by Lee Strasberg and the Actors' Studio. Author of: *An Actor Prepares* and *My Life in Art.*

25. Ballet Review: A non-profit-making US dance journal published by the Dance Research Foundation. It was founded in 1965 by Arlene Croce.

26. Dorothy Bird (1912–96): US dancer, part of Graham's original company.

27. Neighborhood Playhouse: originally founded as an off-Broadway theatre but closed in 1927. Re-opened as the Neighborhood Playhouse School of the Theatre and became closely associated with Sanford Meisner who used Konstantin Stanislavski's System to develop his own technique.

28. Agnes de Mille: (1905–93): US choreographer for ballet, theatre and film. Well known for her choreography for musicals such as Oklahoma and Carousel.

29. *Dancing Inside* (1999): short film made for TV, director Gillian Lacey.

Chapter 10

From Stillness I Could Feel the Energy Begin

Pauline de Groot

Jacky: How did you start dancing?

Pauline: I loved movement as a child and I went to ballet school in Amsterdam when I was 7, my teacher was Nel Roos.[1] When I was 11 she put me in the pre-professional class. I also had modern dance classes but I didn't like the teacher as much. Later my mother and Nel Roos cooked up this idea that I should go to the United States to study modern dance – to be young enough to make a dance career possible, it should be soon. So then I was sent to the States at the age of 15. My training before had been ballet and folk dancing for fun and I played music (flute). I loved folk dancing and different musics. I wasn't too happy with the aesthetic of the ballet: I couldn't get into the pinkness! Also the toe shoes were so painful … Later I decided toe shoes were not for me and I was happy to cut with that part of the pinkness. There always was that question for me about ballet, the aesthetics. But my love of movement and rhythm kept me dancing. Of course being sent to the States was a major event in my life. I didn't want to go away from home; the States didn't attract me. But with so little confidence I didn't know what better to do than what my mother and my teacher told me would be good for me. I didn't want to disappoint them. I was a scared bird wanting to look courageous. So I went to the Graham School[2] and there I started to get into things.

Fergus: What was it like to be in New York at 15?

Pauline: Oh, very difficult but also in many ways fantastic. I learned a lot about life. I made friends that are still dear to me. Underneath it I felt quite lost and didn't want to let on. I tried to act grown up and wanted to become an artist and that sort of carried me through. But being young and from Holland in New York also had its advantages: I had some luck with good people taking care of me. For instance, the families I stayed with and the dancer Lucas Hoving,[3] who was like a concerned elder towards me. I took spartan pride in having to make my own money. I did many odd jobs: babysitting, fashion modelling and a lot of posing for artists/ painters. Often for dear Raphael and Moses Soyer, old Russian Jews, twin brothers, both painting many of my generation's friends and many dancers. They were generous and paid their models well. I also learned a lot about Jewish life in New

Pauline de Groot in her work *Glass Mountain*, 1987. Photograph: Clemens Boon

York. For the first 4 years I was taking class at the Graham School on scholarship, morning and evening and that was what it was about for me. Now that we know about anorexia, one could say that I was like that at the time. Perhaps lucky that we didn't know. But my dance study and fascination for the forms and qualities of this other way of moving, so different from the ballet, would keep my mind working. My diligence was helpful. I needed to continue studying and dancing.

Fergus: How long were you there?

Pauline: Almost 8 years, and of course perspectives started to change. At first at the Graham School, Martha was my big idol. I was also scared of the old lady! After some years of devoted work I discovered there were other things in dance – at Juilliard[4] where I studied with Lucas, through my Labanotation[5] studies and through working summers at Connecticut College Dance Festival. I saw Merce Cunningham[6] and José Limón[7] and began to dance with people. Lucas asked me to be in his company. There I met my friend Nancy Lewis, who later was in the legendary 'Grand Union'.[8] The second half of my 8 years was more alive than the first, which I spent mostly at the Graham School. During the last period at the Graham School I had started to taste other 'schools', which meant that my ambition of getting into the company was actually down the drain. For if you don't stick to one school there, you're out. I learned! I was actually beginning to dance with José Limón and still had my hopes about the Graham company … of course that was totally beyond possibility, it couldn't happen.

Jacky: What is the difference between your relationship with your body then, as opposed to now?

Pauline: Dancing was maybe 50 per cent or more the pleasure of moving, the pleasure of having resilience and breath and also contact … the enjoyment of space. And then the satisfaction of being able to do something – the exhilaration. Like the joys of a child being able to walk an edge, or do handstands … To have a certain mastery, a sensed skill. And now still there is the exhilaration, or the pleasure of moving, of giving oneself a full chance. To expand one's space, through breathing, even though now the body can do less. At least less of the vigorous things: but while the body is more limited on the one hand, on the other there is a deeper knowledge and more scope. One can be more refined. I now enjoy working on details of balance and timing and being present and on doing less and less. This was always an important aspect to me but now it can come into focus more.

I feel lucky that my re-education started with Erick Hawkins[9] and André Bernard.[10] I learnt about sensation from them, an understanding of imagery and sensing. So as not to make form and shape or dramatic expression dictate the body. A movement was there for no particular reason, for the sensed movement itself – quite a revolutionary idea for that time. For me that was closer to meditation. Meditation has been important in why I kept dancing. From stillness I could feel the energy begin: from only breathing, not letting the talking mind take over

Pauline de Groot in her work *Canticle* at the New York YMCA, 1962. Photograph: Vladimir Sladon

and from being in the moment … this somehow has been the inspiration for my dancing.

Fergus: When did your re-education' start?

Pauline: With Erick in 1962. It was interesting because I was dancing with José and was Graham trained and here I was beginning to make my own work; I needed that, now was the time. I had found composition classes with Lucas at Juilliard and with Louis Horst[11] at Connecticut College very difficult. I needed to assimilate, experiment, and I made a solo. That summer my ballet teacher, Nel Roos, paid a visit to Connecticut College. She knew Erick Hawkins. So she asked me to show her my dance and invited Erick and his composer/musician Lucia Dlugochewski. I was pretty nervous. But Erick somehow spotted something in my dancing, something about what I was trying to figure in movement. Something with softening and listening that wasn't in the language of Limón, or anything I had learned before.

Jacky: How old were you at this point?

Pauline: Nineteen. I had been on tour with José Limón and on coming back I felt this big change in life, not knowing what was to come. I felt more adult and inspired. I started to experiment with newly found feelings, sensations in movement. So when Erick spotted something in my work and asked me to come and work with him I was very excited. But then he set about re-educating me and that was quite a blow – having to learn from him as though from the beginning! He would meticulously point out habits, like holding tightness in your leg, or tensions somewhere that I hadn't ever considered. Yet even though he was sometimes obnoxious and could talk the whole rehearsal or class time and more, he was eloquent and knew what he was talking about. I fell in love with this knowledge and wanted to learn more after the initial ego pain. He would speak about Buddhism, Indian philosophy and art; this was wonderful education, the best I had as a dancer. He also sent me to André Bernard, now a well-known specialist of kinesiology education (at New York University), where I would lie on the floor or table and learn about softening and sensing awareness with images through his lightest touch. Erick would send all his dancers to André for re-education in the 1960s.

Fergus: I'm very interested, because I only know of Erick Hawkins as Graham's partner. I'm interested that he had that approach.

Pauline: Yes. At the time Erick was not liked very much in Graham circles, having split from her and gone into this 'softening'. His approach to sensing movement, 'think-feel', and economy of effort I believe came through his work with Barbara Clark, a student of Mabel Elsworth Todd, the author of *The Thinking Body*.[12] I believe André Bernard was also a pupil of Barbara's. Erick really knew the difference between his habits as an ex-ballet dancer and softening and sensing.

Fergus: So what happened then?

Pauline: Working with Erick was night and day – in fact sometimes more night than day. Sometimes he would get us to the studio at 10 in the evening and work us till

4 a.m. It was quite mad. Some years after I'd left I heard that he changed this pattern – lucky for the dancers, but in our time it was far out. But he would also send us to watch Indian dance and look at details and listen to the music. They were definitely exciting years working with Erick … We toured a lot in the United States and went to Paris once. But suddenly for me after an unhappy relationship, I needed to return to Holland. I hadn't seen my brothers for many years while they had grown up. My parents had separated, I needed to know something more about my family. I left all behind in the United States not knowing if I'd ever dance again. Once back in Amsterdam, Nel Roos soon asked me to teach in her school. This actually got me out of a hole for I didn't feel any relationship with the dance I saw in Holland. I had no idea yet what I could do. So the teaching in her school was empowering. She really wanted me to teach traditional Graham technique, which I considered and could possibly have done but didn't want to, after my shift in aesthetics with Erick. Nel Roos also helped get me a first grant from the government – the sum of a thousand guilders to give me a boost to choreograph something. This got me started. She was one of my guardian angels I could say. But later she asked me to stop teaching the 'soft' work in her school. I understood well at the time and left her school; I was expecting a baby and was beginning to build my own school and curriculum, so I was keeping quite busy.

Fergus: How do you train, how do you keep fit? Since that time, have you always been your own trainer? Obviously you've taken things like yoga and different disciplines, but as far as your own work goes, have you trained yourself?

Pauline: Yes. But teaching for nearly 20 years in the Theaterschool[13] was almost like a daily training – I do and I give, I give and I do. The days I would work with my company we would do a warm up more or less focused on the research of the piece. And after the merging of my school with the Theaterschool it became easier for me to drop in to the invited colleagues' and guest teachers' classes and 'brush up', for example with John Rolland[14] and Nancy Topf,[15] Steve Paxton,[16] Nancy Stark Smith[17] and many more. This helped me enormously – to stay in a sort of research mode. Through my teaching I learned how to work. On the floor with the students, they practically taught me. To see the bodies and the specific problems gives the openings to the solutions. You know how this works! For me the breath, gravity, listening to sensations, awareness through doing and not doing – these have been my teachers. Exploration, it would be called now, as part of a rigorous dance training. The forms and patterns in my classes went through various changes over the years. At first T'ai Chi, yoga and Open Theater (New York) work were the essential allies, and from the 1970s also Contact Improvisation, Release, Alexander Technique[18] and later Chi Kung. The principles of economy of effort for the most beautiful and efficient movement are only common sense in these disciplines. This had been inspiration all along – for falling and crumpling as well as for running, jumping or 'busybodyness'.

And lately (again) I've worked with Russell Dumas[19] in my 'time off', in France in his studio and in Australia. He is a phenomenal technician and a wonderful teacher of softness, partnering, spine and precision … this has been a nourishing exchange. I also still roll on the floor and I jog. I do the basics of sitting and breathing, and if there is no space or dance possibility I still do my meridian stretches or Chi Kung; and sometimes in the studio I can 'train' within the dance I am working on, a separate warm-up is not needed.

Jacky: What's interesting for us is the adapting and shifting and finding new ways of working in order to keep going as a performer.

Pauline: I think it is important. I used to think I had to train every day – and somewhere I still think so, but differently. Since I only have the studio every other day while my co-tenant has the other days, I've started to use those days to not dance, to do other things. Besides the production, management, renting or administrative stuff that continues (arrhh!), time for other important things like taking care of my health or being with family or just for hanging out! At present, after a very busy autumn and winter and lots of travelling, teaching and performing I have not danced or even taught for 6 months – for recuperation reasons. I only do my daily yoga and Chi Kung. I seem to need a break! In the coming season I'll begin a simple breathing training again and I plan to teach a class called 'Slowly Slowly' – to move with respect for the (older) body and to research moving slowly. The days of not dancing have given me new energy! It brings me back into the life outside, relationships – my daughter, grandson, neighbours, life is rich.

And about how I train. I used to need to start lying on the floor to let things settle – roll around and stretch and yawn and soften before becoming more specific through centring and releasing the unnecessary. But lately, especially in the mornings, I've needed to do some revving up of energy at the beginning, so I do jogging. The gentle pounding of the run is apparently very good for the bones, protection against osteoporosis and calcium growths, etc. and it is so energizing! I've started classes that way too; a soft jog, first in place to settle the insides, sense the spine and open up … and then into the space – we can do everything while jogging.

Fergus: How long does this process take?

Pauline: It varies. I can go into the studio and go right into moving sometimes, if I am in an easy mode. Sometimes the mode that I'll be working in comes from the street, I have to go with that first. Then after a while I can lie down and do some stretching if I need it – but maybe sometimes I don't need it.

Fergus: And is the stretching normally yoga-related?

Pauline: No. When I say yoga, I mean it in the sense of being quiet, and working with breathing or with weight and softening. Also to practise sitting (meditation) and being aware of posture and/or movement. So it's not a specific brand of yoga. I'm actually not very experienced in a particular yoga.

Fergus: Do you have a specific mode of stretching that you use?

Pauline: Yes, or no! From the basics of André's work and Release I have developed, generally speaking, a lengthening of the outside and collecting and gathering on the inside, helping the alignment. The basic warm up has to do with sensing gravity. I do use principles from all the good stuff I have learned beside dancing: the yoga Sun Salutation, Meridian stretches, Chi Kung warm up, T'ai Chi – with much respect for the specifics. But my ways fluctuate. I don't have one specific mode.

Jacky: It seems to me that part of being a more mature dancer and carrying on is to find some sort of harmony between your training and your life. You've got to, because as you get older, your life tends to become more complicated anyway.

Pauline: Yes, doesn't it! For instance that exercise in the morning, I really need to do. If I forget I'll feel a need half way through the day to stop and do it. It makes a great difference if I do a good set. Sometimes I'll just do a Chi Kung. That's great to do outside – I have a small space on the roof balcony. I prefer to do my evening set when it's dark. I'm a little afraid of the neighbours.

Fergus: I want to ask you about something we were talking about earlier: you've been studying Shiatsu, very seriously, and you said that there was what looked like a conflict between the Shiatsu work and performing. I was interested to hear about that.

Pauline: Well, performing or even making work for others is so intense for me and takes so much of my attention and energy that it is hard to be seriously studying as well. I don't seem to be able to divide myself into two such concentrated areas. That is a conflict. I've tried to divide my days – one day dance and the other day Shiatsu, either working on people or being more into a study mode. Even that is a lot, my energy has been fading. I need to find a way somehow to make the two things swim together. I'm not sure if I can – maybe it will prove impossible!

Fergus: Is there a feeling in you that you might leave one for the other?

Pauline: Now there is a feeling that I might leave all dance and performance. Performance would be the easy one to let go, because I have so many little ailments. On the other hand, some ritual forms and performance of improvisation, when they go well, are so satisfying. It is communication, this may keep me hooked. So I won't be leaving dance to become a Shiatsu practitioner. My role models, Martha, Erick, José, were all performing way past their 60s. But I have to see.

Jacky: The language of your work is very physical and it's dancerly, but you have also chosen to work with text; could you talk about that?

Pauline: I've worked with speaking, text and singing all along. For my piece *V.O.I.D.*, or *Velocity Of Interfering Data*, in 1995/96, there was quite a bit of text. The blurb for it goes like this: [reads] *'Inspired by the vastness of open space, infinity, and the fact that we are only walking around here for a short time, V.O.I.D. could be called an ode to existence. It celebrates the all encompassing n o t h i n g as the background for constantly passing disturbing elements.'* For each performance a special guest was invited who didn't know the piece, to interfere and solo in between us as a 'disturbing factor'. One time it was Christina Svane,[20] not in the role of dancer/performer which she also is, but as storyteller, speaking her own poetry with relevance to the theme. I also used text on tape at different points: poetry of Jerome Rothenberg's, a definition of the 'void ', the Buddhist view on emptiness, a part of a Sutra, my own text, etc. I originally had wanted to speak the texts, but in the end, to be better equipped for dealing with dancers and disturbing elements, I put them on tape. I felt the texts very much made atmosphere for the piece. About my last piece for three dancers including myself and no text, *Pierres de Mousse* (stones of moss) in Helsinki (Side Step Festival, January 2000), an 85-year-old man from the audience who had never seen dance before said, 'to me this is poetry of the body.' I like that very much.

Jacky: Do you think you're getting enough support in terms of money and resources, is this an issue?

Pauline: Yes very much, support is very meagre in the Netherlands, for example for me there has not been support. But the fact that I was invited to dance and teach in Israel with Amos Hetz[21] in November 1999 and to Berlin for a 2-week performance-project with Suprapto's[22] Circulation in September 1999 or to Finland with my little company and teaching, that is support. So there is support, but not specifically in the Netherlands.

Fergus: Has the support here reduced from what it was?

Pauline: Yeah, generally it has reduced. But there are countless more companies applying. And for the division of funds most of the attention is given to the young and up and coming. They don't have a way to deal with older independent people. I'm maybe the only one of the older people who is still performing and also independent. It seems that everyone else 'my age' is either half a generation younger or is associated with some institution or theatre.

Fergus: Could we ask you briefly to continue the chronology where you left off? You came back to the Netherlands, you worked with your old teacher teaching, you got a grant, you started to make work – on from there?

Pauline: In Amsterdam I rented studio space, a classroom of an abandoned school. It was very important to have a place to work. I started to teach so that was the beginning of my independent 'studio'. Through my teaching in the ballet academy I had a good look at what this schooling was like. What I was teaching was very new and different for the students – especially in attitude. Some of them started coming to my classes outside of school … against the rules. I started dreaming of the school I would like if I were a student. Then I got the studio in the Koestraat and my first dance group helped paint the place. From first teaching three or four evenings a week and then also three mornings, I began to develop a curriculum for the day school. We were actively touring and performing at that time. I guess – young and idealistic – we had the energy! When my school got going, I was teaching dance technique and improvisation/composition and a form of yoga or elementary movement, remembering the work with André. The other teachers were Jim Tyler, the father of my daughter (who was born in 1970), teaching dance technique and composition, Jenn Ben Yakov from the New York Open Theater teaching theatre and ensemble, Phoa Ian Tjong, martial movement and later John Yalenezian, T'ai chi and rhythm (drumming!) and there were others.

Then the 'Theaterschool' began to collect all the separate schools and academies in Amsterdam under one umbrella organization. I was invited in 1974 to become a teacher and join the process of creating a new dance department. The two Amsterdam modern dance studios of Bart Stuyf[23] and myself would somehow become absorbed into the main Theaterschool. But as I had just begun my school I was quite reluctant. I believed in the philosophy of my school – that it would train another kind of dancer. To me it was important that the daily dance training should include 'soft' techniques from the beginning and training in sensation, awareness and creative process and also composition and rhythm/music. In other words, creative process and sensation/breathing should be part of the essential dance education, it should not be postponed. This was asking for problems, for the Graham and traditional modern dance teachers from the other affiliated schools were going for a programme of mostly 'hard' techniques and for what looked to me like a kind of mixture of modern dance: some Graham, some Limón, some ballet, some Cunningham. Maybe later some de Groot, or soft techniques, but students would only be allowed to choose and work in 'studios' like mine or Kurt's after this ballet 'basis'. So I needed to resist that. There were some pretty hard fights and misunderstandings to form a modern dance department! Although the school was managing to run with this division in the middle, it took about 10 years to form a dance department with a spine and not afraid of process. Then it became possible to invite people like Steve Paxton, Nancy Stark Smith,[24] Nancy Topf, Marsha Paludan,[25] Simone Forti,[26] John Rolland, eventually even Body-Mind Centering,[27] but also (from the 'Cunningham' side) Albert Reid[28] and Miriam Berns,[29] to mention a few.

Fergus: In those 10 years, was your school part of the Theatreschool, or was it separate?

Pauline: For the first few years it was separate. The students were studying my programme but were also given privileges of Theaterschool students, like student cards and general classes. It only slowly became clear to me that the Theaterschool never wanted my school to be a separate department … at least not officially. But since a new modern dance department was about to be designed I wanted to create a place where my school could also flourish between the other more traditional ideas. This got very complicated! And the 'hard' modern dance techniques were so afraid of being taken over by the 'soft' techniques that we were on enemy terms.

Jacky: So did you decide to withdraw from that at some point?

Pauline: In the heat of the discussion years the department formed a three-headed directorship: Aat Hougée,[30] Bart Stuyf (from the 'hard' side) and myself ('softy').

Aat, the administrative light, helped to juggle the philosophy and organization into a form. He had worked with me and understood the needs of process and 'soft' techniques. It took years of debates (and teaching), but when I felt more confident my vision was protected I was glad to leave the co-directorship. I continued to teach for more than 10 years after. Bart Stuyf also left around that time. Soon after, Jaap Flier[31] joined Aat Hougee as a co-director.

Then in 1989 I took leave as a staff teacher. Although I loved teaching I needed time away from spending most of my energy on students and not having enough left for doing my own thing. In all those years I had been performing and travelling around the world. Around the same time came the great split in the school. Aat had created another school in Arnhem and Mary Fulkerson[32] and many of our core teachers were leaving to teach there. Initially that made me very sad. But the Amsterdam school has proved strong enough – it has survived well with Ria Higler[33] and Trude Cone[34] sharing directorship. Lately it has changed a lot but it still carries on with some of the good old teachers and guests. I have come back occasionally as a guest teacher.

Jacky: What are you working on now, in your life and your work?

Pauline: In my life I'm trying to integrate the study of Chinese meridians, that is Shiatsu[35] and Chi Kung,[36] for my own healing from 'burnout' and for work with others; and integrate my movement work with being grandma – my grandson is now 15-months old – and daily life outside of the studio. These are new priorities! Meditation and following the Buddhist path is part of this. Since my old mother died two years ago and my daughter had a baby I feel I need more time for just being, not doing. And being grandma is a healing in itself – I receive so much from just being with the kid each time. And he is just running away as fast as he can on his little legs, getting grandma to run after him…!

And in my art I would like to work on 'moving slowly', to deepen it. It is what naturally comes up through ageing and through meditation and moving. I have experimented with it in improvisation and performance but I would like to develop something there. I'm not clear yet in what sort of form I could share this work. It is newly inspired by the practice of Chi Kung – the standing still, like a tree. A great training in perception. I don't know if it will make a piece or what – for now it is a study-project.

Jacky: Are you concerned about wider social and political perspectives?

Pauline: I am concerned about our ethical conduct on the planet and I feel urgency about our children – that they learn respect or love for little and big things of life. But in the dance world in Holland I feel very much like an onlooker and when it comes to politics about dance/management or support, a real stranger. In Holland my work is not seen from an understanding of its roots and heritage; the philosophy behind it is not recognized. It's looked at as something phenomenal, personal, the context is not here. When we perform in the United States that suddenly shows up so clearly.

Pauline de Groot in *Sites and Spaces*, 1994. Photograph: Joyce Limburg

Fergus: You were talking earlier about the 'lessening of the personality' and Julyen Hamilton,[37] when we talked to him, quoted Ravi Shankar[38] as saying that to perform is wonderful, but the greatest thing is to teach. Is there a natural progression to some other plane which is not performing? I don't think I believe that, but I'm interested in what you think.

Pauline: I think the ego gets in the way of performing just as it can get in the way of anything else. Somehow to do a good performance you need to be in touch with the spirit of the work, not the ego. The ego has very smart ways of parading like the spirit too. Probably this is true for whatever kind of performance. I think of the ego as the chattering me, who is afraid, who gossips, who is very proud, and wants and wants, is scheming and not very open or philosophical and who tries to be smart, etc. In meditation one takes time to look at this endless activity, without judgement and finds a smile or a great hug, if it comes up, to pacify all that. Often this is not easy at all, not a natural progression – it takes real courage and discipline – to become compassionate. But I believe that it is worth the trouble, so I try …

Amsterdam, The Netherlands, 12 December 1999

Notes

1. Nel Roos: Dutch ballet teacher and choreographer, Director of the Nel Roos Ballet Academy in Amsterdam.
2. Martha Graham School: founded by Martha Graham, great pioneering choreographer of American Modern Dance.
3. Lucas Hoving (1912–2000): Dutch-born dancer, choreographer and teacher, danced with Kurt Joos, José Limón and his own company. Later was Director of the Rotterdam Academy of Dance.
4. Juilliard: New York dance, drama and music school, offering pre-professional conservatory training.
5. Labanotation: system of movement analysis and notation invented by the Hungarian dancer, choreographer and movement theoretician Rudolf von Laban.
6. Merce Cunningham (1919–2009): originally a dancer with Martha Graham, he became one of the most important innovators of post-war American modern dance. He choreographed for his own company from the 1950s up to his death in 2009, collaborating for many years with composer John Cage. The Cunningham technique is taught as a dance style all over the world.
7. José Limón (1908–72): influential US choreographer, originator of his own dance style. He first danced with Doris Humphrey and Charles Weidman, before forming his own company in 1946. Limón technique is still widely taught around the world.
8. *Grand Union* (1971–76): group of New York postmodern dancers who created mainly improvised work in various combinations; the group included Steve Paxton, David Gordon Douglas Dunn, Trisha Brown, Yvonne Rainer, Barbara Dilley, Nancy Lewis, Nancy Green.

9. Erick Hawkins (1909–94): a leading US modern dance choreographer and dancer. He was the first man to dance with Martha Graham's company and was later married to her for some years. He formed his own company and worked to redefine dance technique according to the principles of kinesiology.

10. André Bernard: one of the foremost teachers of Mabel Todd's ideas which make use of visual and tactile-kinesthetic imagery to point the student towards healthier posture and movement. He has been teaching body alignment as a member of the New York University faculty since 1966, as well as teaching annual summer intensives in California and Europe.

11. Louis Horst (1884–1964): composer, choreographer, pianist. He was musical director for the Denishawn company before becoming Martha Graham's musical director and dance composition teacher in her school. He helped define the principles of modern dance choreography and encouraged the use of contemporary music for dance scores.

12. *The Thinking Body* by Mabel Elsworth Todd: an influential book about the mechanics of body action which first proposed the use of visual imagery as an aid to efficient use of the body.

13. The Theaterschool, Amsterdam: an institution which provides full-time training courses in all the theatre arts – acting, dance, mime and circus arts.

14. John Rolland: movement and visual artist and practitioner of release work, based on the kinaesthetic exploration of mental imagery. He was a pupil of Barbara Clark and André Bernard and developed his own approach to release, which he called 'Todd Alignment'.

15. Nancy Topf (1942–98): dancer, choreographer and teacher and a pioneer in the areas of bodywork, release technique and dance improvisation.

16. Steve Paxton: US dancer and teacher, see interview p. 87 and biography p. 192.

17. Nancy Stark Smith: US dancer, teacher and writer, one of the originators, with Steve Paxton, of Contact Improvisation and a long-time editor of the magazine *Contact Quarterly*.

18. Alexander Technique: created by Frederick Matthias Alexander, the method works to change (movement) habits in our everyday activities through re-establishing the natural relationship between the head, the neck and the back. It is a simple and practical method for improving freedom of movement, balance and coordination through re-educating the mind and body.

19. Russell Dumas: dancer, teacher and choreographer who has worked with many prominent companies all over the world and now directs Dance Exchange and the Dancelink Programme in his native Australia.

20. Christina Svane: US dancer, choreographer and poet.

21. Amos Hetz: dancer, choreographer and teacher, is the head of the movement and movement notation department in the Rubin Academy of Music & Dance in Jerusalem and director of Room Dances Festival in Israel.

22. Suryodarmo Suprapto: Javanese artist who first developed Amerta movement practice which draws on perceptions of our relationship with the environment and the natural world. From its Buddhist roots, Amerta movement teaches ways to lessen our sense of identification in life and movement. In 1986 he founded the Padepokan Lemah Putih where Amerta movement is now taught in Java.

23. Bart Stuyf: Bart Stuyf began his career as a modern dancer in the Netherlands in 1961. He went to the United States in 1968 to study with Martha Graham and Merce Cunningham. Upon his return to Amsterdam he founded his own company, the Multi Media Foundation. He now lives and works as a sculptor in the United States.

24. Nancy Stark Smith: US dancer and founding participant in Contact Improvisation. Initially trained as an athlete and gymnast, she has since worked as a dancer, performer, instructor, author

and organizer. In 1975, she founded *Contact Quarterly*, an international journal of dance and improvisation, which she continues to co-edit and produce with Lisa Nelson.

25. Marsha Paludan: US dancer and teacher whose eclectic approach integrates Alexander Technique, Developmental Technique, Yoga, T'ai Chi and Contact Improvisation.

26. Simone Forti: American postmodern choreographer some of whose greatest influences came from observations of children, animals and plants because of her objection to the "isolated, fragmented, and artificial movements" in many formal dance techniques. She was one of the first to incorporate chance procedure, rules/games, improvisation, speaking/singing, and scores, usually in non theatrical environments, as part of dance practice. She is the author of *Handbook in Motion* and many articles.

27. Body-Mind Centering® (BMC℠): Drawing from both Western and Eastern scientific knowledge, Body-Mind Centering is an experiential study of the major body systems – skeletal, muscular, fluid, organ, neuroendocrine – and evolutionary developmental patterns that underlie human movement.

28. Albert Reid: dance educator, performer, former Merce Cunningham dancer and member of the Judson Dance Theater.

29. Miriam Berns: US dancer and teacher, danced with Cunningham and Dan Wagoner.

30. Aat Hougée: Dutch co-director of the School for New Dance Development with Pauline de Groot and Bart Stuyf (later replaced by Jaap Flier), and then co-director with Mary Fulkerson of the European Dance Development Centre in Arnhem.

31. Jaap Flier: Dutch dancer, choreographer and director. After a distinguished career as a dancer, he was director of Australian Dance Theatre and the Sydney Dance Company before returning to the Netherlands and becoming a director of the School for New Dance Development.

32. Mary O'Donnell Fulkerson: US dancer, choreographer and teacher of release-based work, she is a Fellow of Dartington College, United Kingdom, and directed dance schools in the Netherlands and Germany before returning to the United States. She is the author of a book: *Release, Seven Zones of Comprehension Coming from the Practice of Dance.*

33. Ria Higler: Amsterdam-based teacher and performer. She was artistic co-director of the School for New Dance Development from 1989 till 1998.

34. Trude Cone: co-directed the School for New Dance Development (SNDO) in Amsterdam through the 1990s. She is also a Body Mind Centering practitioner and works as a movement therapist.

35. Shiatsu: A traditional hands-on Japanese healing art.

36. Chi Kung or Qigong: the Mandarin Chinese term used to describe various Chinese systems of physical and mental training for health, martial arts and self-enlightenment.

37. Julyen Hamilton: see interview p. 59 and biography p. 191.

38. Ravi Shankar: great Indian sitar player, teacher and popularizer of Indian music in the West.

Chapter 11

Please Come and Dance on the Lotus of my Heart

Bisakha Sarker

Fergus: How did you start dancing?

Bisakha: I can take this question in two parts. One is how I started in India and then how I started in England. I first started to dance because it was my mother's dream that I would dance. She loved dancing, and she was not allowed to dance for social reasons. She went to a missionary school. She remembered doing a 'poppy dance' where all the little children had red tutus, and at the end of the dance they all put their heads with their black hair down in the middle, and their red tutus stood out around this patch of black to make the poppy. I had never seen a poppy in India. So when I first saw a poppy I realized what that dance meant, that was wonderful … oh my Mum's poppy dance! She really wanted to dance – she couldn't but she had the desire. So she wanted both my sister and me to dance, and when young children usually get told fairy stories before going to sleep she used to tell us stories about dancers, and especially about Uday Shankar,[1] whose dance she absolutely loved; and she used to stroke my eyebrows and said 'when you grow up I'll groom them and you can go and dance in Uday Shankar's school.' She would also take me to see good dance performances. When I was very young I saw the Bolshoi and various other companies. Only now I know what a privilege that was.

Fergus: This was in Calcutta?

Bisakha: Yes. We used to get lots of major companies in Calcutta. She made sure that I got an opportunity to learn dance, so that's how I started. I knew that I would have to study and do the usual things of going to the university – not that I did that reluctantly, I was quite happy to do that but I made sure that I continued my dance training. Most of the people of the middle-class society in Calcutta practised one form of art or another. Saturdays and Sundays were our days for going to art schools. There were a number of different schools in ordinary school buildings which opened for dance classes on Saturdays and Sundays. I learnt from a very early age from someone called Basanta Singh – he used to teach a style of dancing called Manipuri.[2] He was also very keen on performance; I suppose in those days dancers had to survive by putting shows together – like we do – and as soon as he

Bisakha Sarker solo performance in 2007. Photograph: Simon Richardson got a few students he would push them into all kinds of shows. I was quite tall for my age, so though I was very young I got pushed into those group dances – to fill the stage! I think that was a wonderful experience for me – performing right from a very early age.

Fergus: What kind of age?

Bisakha: Definitely before 9. We would have rehearsals in somebody's house, it was an extremely safe environment. Calcutta is very vibrant for this sort of cultural activity which could be called community dance; this came from Tagore's[3] influence – he wrote so many beautiful dance dramas, so that dance could evolve. He especially wrote them to promote dancing – he was a great believer in dance. It was almost a measure of one's cultural sophistication to know Tagore's songs and to dance to them; it was also very fashionable for young girls to get involved in this sort of thing, it showed that you belonged to a cultured society.

So we used to do quite a lot of these performances. Some of them in quite ridiculous situations, on some made-up stage in the middle of nowhere … travelling by train, getting out of a bus … the whole interesting side of dancing that one gradually learns as one tours with companies. So I learnt in Calcutta through these schools; I learnt mostly classical dance styles, and this Tagore dance form which combined various styles. These were mostly music- and theme-based dances. What we danced was not a particular technique but the meaning of the words. The communication of the emotion was the motivation.

The dance dramas were based on love stories of one kind or another and within that there was also an element of dealing with social issues such as untouchability, conviction of one's own religious belief and women's rights: there is a wonderful story of a princess who wasn't very beautiful and was rejected by her lover; so she becomes very beautiful and wins him back, but then at the end says 'No, I can't be with you if you don't treat me as your equal; only if we can work as left hand and right hand will I come to you.'

Lots of modern thoughts there!

After that, when I was in the university, I went to Uday Shankar's school; that was a major change for me. Until then I saw dance as something where you dress up and dance to all those romantic songs, looking beautiful. But when I went to Uday Shankar's school for the first time, I understood that dance is actually a whole art form: lots of important things happen – it is not just the body moving with music. The awareness of costume, lighting, stage presence, choreography, all those things came together; I saw dance as a serious subject.

I was also deeply influenced by another dancer who has done a great deal of modern work called Manjusri Chaki-Sircar.[4] She had a similar type of training to mine, but more extensive, and she kept on learning and developing new techniques. Manju-di, as we called her, was doing really interesting work with Tagore's music. At that time she was living in America and was very influenced by

Martha Graham's work. She was a huge influence on me in terms of choreography as well as expression in dance. For example, she would say 'why does one always have to smile, one always dances with a fixed smile, that's not how one feels all the time, so why does one have to do that in dance?' She would come occasionally from the States to Calcutta and we would do loads of exciting work – I think this was around the late sixties. Once she came back and we choreographed one piece where we were lying on the floor working with our arms; on the day of the performance we had to leave that one out because it would have been too radical and challenging – three girls lying on the floor to dance!

Our school, Uday Shankar India Culture Centre, always had visitors from abroad; whenever American dance groups were travelling to India they would come to our school. This was often because of Uday Shankar's connection with the impresario Sol Hurok[5] and the phenomenal success of his tours of America. We were so fortunate when Paul Taylor[6] visited; the company came to see our work and we all worked back stage and were able to see the company from so close. Then Pauline Koner[7] visited and we did workshops with her; our teacher would also encourage us to present our work: I remember how interesting and inspiring it was when we prepared and presented a piece for Pauline Koner and listened to her lectures. In this centre I was not only learning to dance, I was also being trained to think about dance in an analytical way and present it.

Jacky: Did you do class and study specific techniques?

Bisakha: The classes were all in different styles; I first started with Manipuri style, then I learnt some Bharatanatyam,[8] Kathakali[9] and Kuchipudi.[10] In the Uday Shankar Centre I had to learn three classical styles – Manipuri, Bharathnatyam and Kathakali – those classes you took just as classical classes should be, you didn't use your imagination to change the choreography or technique, you just followed the rules. Then there was a fourth class, which we called general class, where we learnt the Uday Shankar style. This was actually an improvisation class. That is why I feel very uptight when people say there is no improvisation within Indian dance culture. In our improvisation classes, we always started with walking, that was our warm up, and gradually things would be added – swing your arms, dip your body – gradually the walk would become a dance, through instruction. We were also so fortunate – we had a whole orchestra for every dance class: a percussion instrument, a stringed instrument, a flute and a water xylophone, so we were getting such a wonderful training in musicality.

Fergus: Would these musicians also play for technique classes?

Bisakha: Not all of them. We would have the percussion – a tabla player – or the teachers could also play. The usual classes were often done with a wooden stick just keeping the rhythm.

Jacky: That simple walking device leading into dance, so brilliantly simple – where did that come from?

161

Bisakha: Uday Shankar always did it, I don't know where he got that from, I believe that's the way they did it in his Almora school[11] which he started, probably about 60 or 70 years ago. Uday Shankar started his dancing career with Pavlova.[12] He was a young student in London, learning painting with Rothenstein[13] at the Royal College. Pavlova had just done a tour of India and Japan, and she did a performance in Covent Garden to raise funds for a flood that had happened in Japan. In it she included a Japanese dance and an Indian dance called *Oriental Impression*. Somebody saw that and suggested that she could ask this young man, Uday Shankar (who was performing Indian dance at society events, as well as painting), to perform with her. So Pavlova brought him into her company and she absolutely loved him. He choreographed two pieces for her, one was a duet called *Radha Krishna* for himself and Pavlova, and the other *Hindu Marriage*, which was for the company. Pavlova wanted Uday Shankar to go with her on her American tour, so she went to Rothenstein and rumour has it that she said to him 'You don't need a body like that to be a painter – he belongs to me!' So that wonderful body came to the world of dance.

After that tour, he left Pavlova's company and went on to form his own company and toured to England and Paris. He met Simki,[14] a pianist who soon started to dance with him. They became legendary dance partners. I guess at that time, in the 1920s, the piano must have been his accompaniment for dance – so Indian dancing to western music and western instruments is not something that has just been invented! Afterwards he also got funds, I think, from the Elmhirsts[15] at Dartington who gave him a large sum of money to start a school in Almora. He prepared some of his pieces at Dartington. Lisa Ullman[16] was there at the same time. When I met Lisa Ullman, she asked me about him and that was the first time that my worlds of dance in India and here got connected. Until then, nobody understood when I said I worked in Uday Shankar's style of creative dance. I feel a part of that whole tradition and heritage, of breaking the boundary and moving across. When he had to teach dancers in Pavlova's company, he must have faced the same problem that I face when I go to a school to teach Indian dance to children without any previous experience of the style.

In La Meri's book *Total Education in Ethnic Dance*,[17] she dedicates it to 'The pioneers of the golden age of modern dance' and Uday Shankar is named as one of them. He started a new style of dance. He did what I call 'free dance', he started to make dances on many new themes, some traditional, some contemporary – Indian dance started to be based not on myths of gods and goddesses. For example, he created *Labour and Machinery*, which was an amazing piece, a commentary on industrialization. He made fascinating machine-like movements, all based on Indian dance movements, combining classical dance steps with innovative use of arms and torso. What he said was that he did not take any technique from western dance. He said 'I have learnt showmanship from the West, but I have kept the spirit of the dance purely Indian.'

It's so difficult to teach aesthetics: there is no step-by-step guide to follow; it's a kind of intuitive learning. That is why in his dance training schemes he kept classical dance at the heart of it. So as you learn classical dance, somehow you understand or maybe get a sense of the ground rules of the aesthetics of the specific style. Then you can move in or out of it more confidently and maintain an artistic coherence. Creating a new movement wasn't about combining Indian and western dance movement or putting together different motifs from different styles. We were given full freedom to create new movements using our imaginations, drawing resources if necessary from sections of taught sequences along with any individualistic patterns that our bodies wished to generate. We were given different patterns of Indian music to form these movements into dance motifs.

I finished university, where I was studying statistics. Then I took up the job of teaching physics and maths in a school. The Anthropological Survey of India wanted to do some dance research and they wrote to Uday Shankar, who recommended me for the post of senior research fellow. That was a wonderful opportunity to look at dance as an academic subject, as something that is different from going out to dance. So I worked as a dance research fellow, doing my research mainly in the rural areas around Calcutta and looking at the folk/classical continuum – when does a folk dance become classical? The area where I did my field research had three groups of dance practitioners. Firstly the Nachnis who were really folk singers – they had their own special patrons. Although they were prostitutes they were quite respected for their singing. They often danced while singing their songs. Then there were the Natuas, who did lots of acrobatic work, and dances of animals. Most of the Natuas were farmers or hired firm workers. Finally there were companies of Chhau dancers, which is a much more developed dance drama form.

Jacky: Did you write up your research?

Bisakha: No I did not complete the work. Just one paper was published in the journal of *The Anthropological Survey of India*. That was about a system of analysis I was thinking of at that time. I didn't know Labanotation[18] and didn't know how such an analysis could take place, I was starting from scratch. The title of the paper was *Objective Study of Dance*. The anthropologists involved in different projects were going to various places and collecting really exciting material, but there was no systematic recording of this information, so I was also trying to create some questionnaires for them so that they could produce material that was consistent.

Then I got married and came here to England and all dance disappeared! I almost had to build myself up again completely. That was in 1971. I didn't come here with a clearly established identity, and I didn't realize that until quite late. Not dancing was so irritating – it was such a vibrant world of dance that I had left behind, I came here and suddenly faced a situation where all day there was nothing around, no work and nobody to talk to. Once I asked somebody what I should read and they looked at me and said 'You could read Charles Dickens.' I was so devastated, I thought to myself 'Is that what people are reading now, in England? I'd better go back to India!' My husband is a doctor, we were staying in an isolated hospital flat with no other families nearby – it was just one flat in the middle of the X-ray department.

Then we came to Liverpool and I started working in an insurance company. One day I saw an advertisement for an Asian programme in a local paper, so I went there with my little girl and told them about my dance background. Through that I got one or two connections. Then I came across a group of Asian people who were getting their acts together to set up an organization to promote annual Asian religious and cultural events. As a part of that program the organizers arranged a cultural evening and they asked me to dance. Soon after that one of the organizers asked me to dance in a toy library, and that was where I met Irene Dilkes.[19] She liked what I did and took me to I M Marsh College[20] where I ran some workshops and classes, so in a way that was my first entry to the serious world of dance in this country. At the same time I became a friend of Spiral Dance Company[21] and got to know Tim Lamford.[22]

All of these people have made such wonderful contributions to my life.

I was working full time so I could only do creative work at the weekends. I had a young child too; but I took her to everything. Since then many dancers have told me how good that was, it made them realize it is possible to have a child and keep on dancing. I had no choice, there was nowhere to leave her. I remember taking her to The Empire and telling them that I wanted her to see good dance from childhood and if she made any noise I would come out; however, if they were to refuse us entry, then they would lose another member of their future audience. That was the first time we saw Wayne Sleep,[23] he was dancing in the group, but it was impossible not to notice him! My daughter was then only 2 or 3 years old. When my second child was still a baby, I was asked to go to Newcastle to dance. They asked me what were my requirements, and without thinking I said 'A cassette player and a bag of disposable nappies.'

Jacky: It would be interesting to collect these stories of dancing mothers! Did you get your disposable nappies?

Bisakha: I did, as well as a child minder for the evening. So this is how I continued dancing. Also for myself I had to feel relaxed. Dance is an important part of my life. I wanted my daughters to grow up sharing my whole life with me.

Jacky: What would your programmes consist of? You would do a solo show of pieces choreographed by yourself?

Bisakha: Most of the pieces are choreographed by me. That is where, again, the training from Uday Shankar's school was very useful because I think of it as a whole programme. I would plan the pieces in a way that makes it easier for me to change costumes, and I would prepare pieces of costuming so that I could add something

Bisakha Sarker dancing in the 1970s.
Photograph: Ray Clarke

and take it off easily. My preparation for dance involves more ironing than actual dancing! I have to put the costumes in a certain order – that is an essential part of dancing for me. I will start with the prayer piece, about 8–10 minutes, and very often I ask hosts to do their introduction after I have done the first piece, so that I have time to change quickly. Usually the programmes won't be more than 40–60 minutes, so I'll have a few pieces, starting almost always with a prayer, then moving into a story piece and one or two pure dance pieces in between. It was very common in those days to have summer play schemes, dance residencies or a week of dance, where I would do Indian dance, Kate Flatt[24] would do East European folk dance, Spiral or Liz Bruin[25] would do contemporary dance, and there might be Spanish dancing, we were all billed together.

In the early 1980s, Gillian Clarke,[26] who was then working for Merseyside Arts, had seen me here and there, and she asked me to become a member of the Dance Panel along with Veronica Lewis[27], Liz Bruin and others. Until then, there had been no black member on Merseyside Arts Dance Panel. So I said, yes, I'll join. And that was very good for me to meet all those people on an equal basis. If I had just stayed within the Indian community, I would perhaps have developed more as a community-based dancer and maybe more in technique, but I wouldn't have had an idea of where to place my dance.

Around that time Cy Grant[28] used to run the Concord Festival, a multicultural festival, and he did one in Liverpool – for which Nahid Saddiqui,[29] Delado Dance Company,[30] Flora Gatha, a beautiful Odissi dancer (currently based in France) and I danced at the Royal Court Theatre. So through that I was being seen and making connection with different people. One day Gillian asked me whether as a member of the Panel, I would like to attend Indian Dance in Britain, a conference at the Commonwealth Institute in London organized by Tara Rajkumar[31] and the Academy of Indian Dance. That was wonderful, after many years I felt that I was breathing again – there was this world of dance! I came back all excited. When I met her next, Gillian asked: 'Would you like to do that all the time? Would you give up your job to take a post as an animateur?' I had never thought about it, I was just struggling with the emotional stress of this awful insurance job. I was also suffering with horrible racist attitudes at work, which I was refusing to acknowledge – I really didn't believe it was happening, having been brought up in India as a member of the mainstream society I could not recognize the obvious signs of institutional racism. You think it can't happen to you. Until then I'd never taken a risk for my dance – artistically, yes, but not with my life. So that was my opportunity and I gave up my job to become the first Asian dance animateur. Since then I have never looked back. I didn't grow up thinking I would take up dance as a full-time profession; dance was just for my soul, as my mum said: 'Get a job to support yourself and leave dance for an escape to sanity!'

Fergus: How do you feel differently now, as a dancer, from when you first started dancing?

Bisakha: I think when I danced before, it was as if I had a life which was flowing in its own way and was occasionally being touched by dance. Now the world of dance has completely entered my life; I cannot separate my life and my dance any more.

Jacky: How has that manifested itself through your performance, do you think?

Bisakha: I think the performances are much stronger and more sincere. At one time it was almost like putting a dress on and now it feels as if it is my skin. That's how I feel. Looking back, I could say that it was always a wonderful sensation to dance, but now it has a different intensity. You devote everything you've got to the dance and there's a certain awareness of total sincerity in that.

Fergus: How do you feel physically, in your body, now, as opposed to when you were a younger dancer?

Bisakha: When I was younger, I was much more conscious of my body and the deformities of my body – all the bad things. I was always worried about a flat nose and I thought if only I had a sharper nose! I used make up colours to make it look sharper!

Fergus: I always tried to make mine look wider!

Bisakha: And then I was very conscious of my hips, and heaviness, so I would never turn my back, I would almost try to find a choreography where I wouldn't have to turn at all. Those were the problems then. But now the problems are different. I've got very bad knees, so getting up and down is harder, yet in general in dance these days I'm going down and up much more than before – as a wonderful young student of mine put it, 'You carry your weight well.' This has made me realize that weight is not simply an issue of mass and shape; it is also about how it is handled in the dance.

As one grows older one has less to prove, physically. I get breathless more easily; I cannot do many movements that I could do before, especially the faster ones. On the other hand I have discovered ways of executing movements that I was not previously aware of. I met a sculptor who is very beautiful, but she has a well-rounded figure. She felt horrible, ugly and embarrassingly fat. She rang me and said: 'I've got a poem, I want somebody to dance it for my graduate show.' Usually for those kinds of phone messages you say, thank you, but try someone else. However on this occasion, I don't know why, but I felt curious and I went to see her. I asked her 'What is it that you are looking for?' She read me the poem; I didn't know how to dance it, so I told her: 'This is a dance only you can do.' She replied 'I don't dance, although I've always wanted to.' I proposed to her that we should try to choreograph it and if it did not work that would be my failure as a choreographer. We started on those terms. We managed to create a unique piece of work that made both of us happy. I had to find the sculptor's language to tell her what I was looking for and then we were able to work together. Her body could move, without self-consciousness. So once when I said: 'I feel so fat,' she said 'Don't say that. You have taught me how to handle that feeling and now I don't feel fat anymore.'

In the early days there was that tremendous need to look beautiful that was more important than being true to the demands of the dance. I felt embarrassed to do awkward movements. Now I want to explore the darker emotions of human life through dance and I wouldn't have had the courage to even think about making a piece about that, earlier on.

Fergus: How do you keep fit? Do you train?

Bisakha: I like to do swimming, that keeps me moving, and I also do some yoga exercises. If I can't find time to do it for myself, I include some of the exercises in classes I teach. Fortunately I am teaching in schools and community settings almost every day, and throughout the day I am physically moving, though that doesn't stretch me the same way a dance technique class would.

Jacky: Do you have a studio space to work in?

Bisakha: No. I work at home. I think I have developed the technique of finding that space within no matter what physical space I'm working in. Because I've always had to work with children and family around me, balancing my artistic and domestic life, I don't need a big space, I don't need a studio space, even within my little room I can practise. As I say, more and more, dancing and life are getting mixed with each other, so in the middle of some other work I'll do a bit of dancing, a little bit of footwork – but that is not pure concentrated technique practice. That I don't do on a regular basis. However, when I make new pieces for my solo performance I go to a most inspiring T'ai Chi Studio in Manchester and when I work with my colleague Sanjeevini[32] to create new productions for our dance company, Sanchari, we use studio spaces in London.

Every time I go to Calcutta – and lately it has been almost once a year, I go to my teacher and I practise with him. Maybe not more than 10 days or so, but that's a rich time. I have to go there early, 6 or 7 o'clock, and have to sit there for about 2 or 3 hours while he gets ready, but he keeps talking, telling things that are so wonderful. So I have learnt that patiently waiting is also part of dance training! Then once it starts, he won't stop and I'm looking at the clock – I've got to go to this place or that place – and he will say 'No, no, stay a bit longer!' Every time I go, I ask him if we can do the first few movements and I think he feels a bit sorry for me now that for the last 20 years I've just been going over the same thing all the time! By then most people would have learnt about ten dance items. Every time he says 'I'm going to teach you this item' - each piece of dance is often referred to as an 'item' – and I show no interest; I just like to do the practice, because I can't tell him that I'm not going to perform those classical pieces. I go to train in this classical style, really just to build my own resources, fitness and strength and to stay in touch with the discipline of classical dance.

Also, lately I have started to do a particular prayer: if you say this in words, it sounds very big, but it's just getting a little bit of time before starting the day to stop and think in a different way. My teacher has taught me a Siva stotra,[33] which is beautiful, it says 'Please come and dance on the lotus of my heart.' [*Bisakha demonstrates*] This hand is the leaping deer – life, and this hand is the thunderbolt – death. It's constantly balancing life and death. So the second time, the life gesture becomes the trident – death, and the death becomes the drum that Nataraj[34] holds and plays. So the hand changes and life changes into death. And the fourth one is 'Lift the veil of illusion': it shows Siva's hair, and from that flows a holy river. But what it is saying is that as the river forms a waterfall, mists are created and that is 'the mist in front of my eyes – please come and dance inside my heart and lift the mist, so that I can see through.' And the last one is 'Liberate me from death'. So I have decided that instead of saying other prayers, I will just dance those five. It has got a step and a rhythm; and sometimes I can't keep that rhythm, but I'm aware that I haven't done it and I think that awareness is also a kind of training. When I was in the insurance company and was not doing any dancing, I remembered something that Uday Shankar said: I showed him some of my drawings and he said 'You always draw yourself.' So I used to draw and that was my dance exercise. All my doodles were dance shapes, and I almost felt I had danced those movements.

Jacky: What are your current objectives in work?

Bisakha: Currently, I work as a freelance artist, doing education work in schools, through the multi-cultural education route. The majority of my work entails doing 1-day sessions. I try to leave a sense of musicality and quality with the children. I am quite fascinated by the language of teaching. The quality comes very much from the proper use of language in teaching. I also work with people with disabilities, any age. There is a general lack of knowledge and awareness about how South Asian dance can be used for and by disabled people.

Returning to the issue of older dancers, it is a tricky one and a huge emotional change to handle as well: sometimes it is possible to lose heart and confidence, and as a performer if you lose confidence in yourself, there is very little to draw from. With age it seems necessary to change the dance, the definition of dance, the pattern of dance. The dance needs to suit the changing needs of the body. It is no good to try to do dances that the body can no longer cope with.

Jacky: Do you think there is a certain quality of dancing you can't do until you are old enough?

Bisakha: That is a very common concept of Indian dance – you don't start to dance unless you are over 40. That's when you start to dance. All the great masters are really those who could dance with only one eyebrow. That is why Indian dancers have danced that long; there are three sections of dance called nritta, nrittya and natya. The first is pure dance – technique-based movement and music together; the second one is movement but working more with the content, maybe dancing a song so there is more meaning coming through; and the last one is working with expression and acting, using mime skills. As one matures, one starts to perform more of the last category of dance: the expressive storytelling mode which requires control of muscles and depth of feeling to communicate a message. So one starts to dance with the body first and then moves on to dance with the soul and energy and whatever is left – so you will look more deeply into what you have.

Liverpool, UK, 9 June 2000

Notes

1. Uday Shankar (1900–1977): Indian dancer in Calcutta (now Kolkata), choreographer and teacher, founded the Uday Shankar India Culture Centre.
2. Manipuri dance: one of the major Indian classical dance forms. It originates from Manipur, a state in north-eastern India.
3. Gurudev Rabindranath Tagore: Indian mystic, poet, painter and Nobel Laureate for literature.
4. Manjusri Chaki-Sircar: dancer and choreographer who was a leader in the development of a modern or New Dance genre in India, examining and re-interpreting the role of women in traditional Indian dance. She founded the Dancers' Guild, a choreographic laboratory and training centre.
5. Sol Hurok (1888–1974): Russian-born US impresario who represented Mikhail Fokine, Anna Pavlova and Galina Ulanova among many others and managed tours to the United States of Diaghilev's Ballets Russes and the Bolshoi Ballet, as well as numerous musicians and theatre companies.
6. Paul Taylor: distinguished US modern dancer and choreographer, founded his own company in 1954 and has remained at the forefront of modern dance ever since.
7. Pauline Koner (1912–2001): US dancer, choreographer and teacher, famous for her solo performances and later as 'permanent guest artist' with the José Limón Dance Company.
8. Bharatanatyam: classical Indian dance form originating in Tamil Nadu and drawing inspiration from the sculptures of the ancient temples of Chidambaram.
9. Kathakali: a highly stylized classical Indian dance-drama noted for the attractive make-up of characters, elaborate costumes and detailed gestures.
10. Kuchipudi: a classical Indian dance form from Andhra Pradesh, India. It is also popular all over South India.
11. The Uday Shankar Academy of Music and Dance: it was founded by Uday Shankar in 1938 and still continues: in 2010 it moved to a new building in Fatsima, near its original site in Almora.
12. Anna Pavlova (1881–1931): early twentieth-century Russian ballerina, toured the world with her company for many years, probably popularizing ballet more widely than any other individual.
13. Sir William Rothenstein (1872–1945): artist and principal of the Royal College of Art, London, in the 1920s.
14. Simki: French ballet dancer who followed Uday Shankar back to India in the 1920s, learnt Indian dance and became Shankar's professional and personal partner.

15. The Elmhirsts: Dorothy and Leonard Elmhirst, philanthropists who founded the Dartington Hall Trust in 1925 and, influenced by Tagore, made it a centre for radical social and artistic experiment.
16. Lisa Ullman (1907–85): assistant and disciple of the great pioneer and dance theorist Rudolf von Laban, she was for many years the principal of the school founded by Laban in Addlestone, Surrey, the Art of Movement Studio, which was the precursor of today's Laban Centre.
17. La Meri: (1898–1988): United states-born Russel Meriwether Hughes later came to be known as 'La Meri', the dancer, poet, writer, ethnic dance teacher and choreographer. Travelling to India, she learnt Bharatanatyam and Kathak dance styles. She analysed dance movement and created a methodology for teaching varied dance forms from different countries..
18. Labanotation: a form of dance notation invented by Rudolf von Laban.
19. Irene Dilks (1942–2000): UK dancer and teacher, original member of London Contemporary Dance Theatre and founder of Spiral Dance Company in Liverpool, she later taught dance at I M Marsh College in Liverpool.
20. I M Marsh College: part of Liverpool John Moores University in South Liverpool, UK, and home to the faculty of Education, Community and Leisure.
21. Spiral Dance Company: innovative regional and touring company based in Liverpool in the late 1970s and 1980s.
22. Timothy Lamford: UK dancer and choreographer, Director of Spiral Dance Company for 6 years in the 1980s and currently a teacher and lecturer in dance and T'ai Chi.
23. Wayne Sleep: UK dancer, originally a principal with the Royal Ballet, he left to pursue a career as a freelance producer of popular dance shows and as an actor.
24. Kate Flatt: UK choreographer whose work frequently draws on folk dance forms. Also a prolific choreographer for opera and theatre.
25. Liz Bruin: dance animateur and lecturer, long active in the North West of England.
26. Gillian Clarke: influential arts administrator who has worked for individual artists, regional arts boards and local authorities since the 1970s.
27. Veronica Lewis: as a dance animateur, she founded Cheshire Dance Workshop and later became Principal of the London Contemporary Dance School.
28. Cy Grant (1919–2010): singer and songwriter, early apologist for West Indian music and arts in the United Kingdom.
29. Nahid Saddhiqi: Indian dancer of the Kathak style, based in the West Midlands of the United Kingdom.
30. Delado Dance Company: Liverpool-based Afro-Caribbean company.
31. Tara Rajkumar: UK-based Barathnatyam dancer, she founded the Academy of Indian Dance in London (now Akademi).
32. Sanjeevini Dutta: Indian dancer and choreographer trained in the Odissi style in Bombay and now director of Kadam, based in Bedford.
33. Siva Stotra: in Hinduism, a stotra is a hymn of praise. These hymns extol aspects of the divine, such as Devi, Siva or Vishnu.
34. Nataraj: the dancing form of Lord Shiva, is a symbolic synthesis of the most important aspects of Hinduism and the summary of the central tenets of this Vedic religion. The term 'Nataraj' means 'King of Dancers'.

Chapter 12

Your Body Knows a Lot of Things

Fergus Early

Fergus Early with Lisa Celisse and Will Palmer in *Jack Be Nimble*, 2002, by Green Candle Dance Company. Photograph: Hugo Glendinning

Jacky: What made you start dancing?

Fergus: I'm told that I saw my two older sisters dancing at our local dancing school and probably at a dancing competition and said that I wanted to do that. In fact I remember my mother taking me to dancing when I was about 4 and I didn't like it at all – they were doing Mickey Mouse's tea party and I ran and hid in the toilet and my mother was very annoyed. But then about a year later, when I was 5, I asked to go, and I went and I evidently enjoyed it.

Jacky: And what was it you enjoyed?

Fergus: I don't know really. I don't remember too much about my early lessons – there was a teacher called Hinemoa Muirhead, a tall and rather serene lady in flat-soled sandals who would do very beautiful demonstrations of ballet positions, very carefully. I think quite soon after I started dancing I went in for one of the local dancing competitions and I remember doing a Tyrolean dance with a horn that my mother had brought back from Switzerland and I'd pretend to blow it. I was wearing shorts with braces and a little hat with a feather. I did a slapping sequence on my thighs – a sort of Schuhplattler[1] – and I think I enjoyed the performing very much.

There was a lot at the dancing school: there was ballet and tap and modern and Greek (a sort of Isadora Duncan-derived movement system, all taken from Greek friezes). I enjoyed doing all the variety of things. And then in the competitions we'd do ballet and tap and modern and something called demi-caractère, where you assumed a character and did a dance based around that character. I remember when I was about 7 or 8 doing a goalkeeper's dance and I also remember doing a rock'n'roll dance in a long stripy T-shirt; that was when Rock Around the Clock came out.

From a very early age dancing was inextricably bound up with performing for me. I think I felt at home on stage right from the start. And I was successful, which presumably helped – I won competitions and things. I suppose I was quite good and also I was a boy, which was a rarity and that was to be an advantage then and throughout my early career.

Jacky: So when did it become clear that you wanted to become a professional dancer?

Fergus: Well, I think the basic decision was taken when I was 10. My sister Teresa,[2] who was a keen dancer and choreographer herself, suggested to my mother that I should audition for the Royal Ballet School, which I did, and I was offered a place.

Jacky: So you did a full ballet training and eventually joined the Royal Ballet Company; what was that experience like?

Fergus: I remember on my first tour I spent most of my time doing old men, putting on lots of make-up and wigs and doddering about the stage, or being a huntsman in *Swan Lake* – just walking across the stage with a cross-bow. Not doing very much dancing, in other words. But I also very shortly joined the newly formed Ballet for All[3] company, which meant that I was one of two dancers who went out from the main company with Peter Brinson[4] and did these lecture demonstration performances. With Ballet for All, I was doing most of the solos and pas de deux from big ballets like *La Fille Mal Gardée*,[5] which are really hard, virtuoso dances. It was very interesting, though. The performing experience was on small stages and often very intimate so you had lots of responsibility. I carried on working with Ballet for All in parallel to dancing with the main company and Peter Brinson gave me my first opportunities to choreograph in a professional context. I also got the opportunity to work with and direct actors as Ballet for All's productions got more elaborate and Peter wrote his 'ballet plays' around the history of dance and so on.

Jacky: You left the Royal Ballet after 6 years when you were 24; why did you leave, and where did you go?

Fergus: I basically left because I wanted to choreograph, but I couldn't see how I could work with the language of classical ballet and the expectations of a ballet company. For example, I always felt very unhappy trying to choreograph for pointe shoes. I really needed to absorb some other approaches to dance and theatre and through the late 1960s we'd had all the major modern dance companies from America in London – Graham, Cunningham, Nikolais, Paul Taylor, Alvin Ailey and so on and I was really inspired by them. So I applied for a grant from the Gulbenkian Foundation[6] to spend some time at the Royal Shakespeare Company observing Peter Hall directing and some time at the London Contemporary Dance School as a kind of study period. Out of this, I struck up a good relationship with Pat Hutchinson,[7] the principal of the London Contemporary Dance School and she offered me a job teaching ballet and the freedom to take any classes I wanted. It was a very good time to be there – not so much for the dance experience, because the Graham technique, which was the main technique at that time, didn't very much agree with me, but creatively it was marvellous. There were some extraordinary people there as students, like yourself, Sally Potter[8] from a film background, Di Davies[9] from a visual arts background and lots more, doing very radical and exciting work with almost endless opportunities to put things on stage or in the studios and other spaces around the building. It was pretty anarchic, but a perfect antidote to 6 years with a ballet company.

Jacky: And then in the mid-70s you left the London Contemporary Dance School. Why was that?

Fergus: Well, I think there was a bunch of us who felt we needed our own space to explore a lot of questions we had. Technical questions, political questions, creative questions.

Fergus Early as Albrecht with Sue MacLennan (on right) as Giselle and Jacky Lansley as Queen of the Wilis in *I, Giselle*, 1981.

So that's what X6 Dance Space[10] was all about. I think it was at X6 that I completed the re-education I began when I left the Royal Ballet.

Jacky: Was part of that process studying other, alternative techniques in depth?

Fergus: Yes, so for example some of the things that have touched me quite deeply I encountered at that time: particularly Mary Fulkerson's[11] work and contact improvisation[12] in various ways. It's an interesting question whether I've studied them in depth. What I've done is to have acquaintance with these forms in workshops and so on, and then I've used them a lot, in teaching and in choreographing, until they became very much part of me and what I do.

Jacky: You also picked up some Yoga, didn't you?

Fergus: I picked up some Yoga… I have a sort of accumulation of things that I've made my own and that have become part of my own training and my own teaching. And in teaching I've found out more about them. And now I have a way of moving that is mine.

Jacky: And has all that work fed into the work you do with Green Candle?[13]

Fergus: In a way, everything I've ever done has fed into the work with Green Candle from Peter Brinson's ballet plays and the sheer theatricality of the ballet, through all the experimentation and iconoclasm. It's all given me lots of tools to address the company's major concern, which is how to make and practise dance that is relevant to its social context but still retains the adventure of art.

Jacky: And you continue to perform with Green Candle?

Fergus: Yes, though not in all the productions. I have performed in our two most recent shows but it is hard to commit to long tours when there is all the business of running the company and all its activities. I can't really envisage *not* performing though – it's something to do with its sheer intensity and focus which is unlike most other things I do.

Jacky: How do you feel differently now than when you first started dancing professionally?

Fergus: Well, when I was about 14, I injured my knee – I was doing a grand jeté in class and it just went. I was actually working on an unsprung, parquet floor. I carried that injury through my student days and into the first 2 or 3 years as a professional before I managed to find a way of working through it, and it eventually went. And I remember that being quite a problem at times. I would be off performances, sometimes, and wearing knee supports and trying to find ways of 'saving' it. When I think about it as a start to my career, it was not all that auspicious. It wasn't wholly incapacitating, I didn't stop altogether at any time, but I had some pretty bad times with it and a lot of pain and worry.

So now that I'm much older and I carry, not a huge amount, but a number of physical problems that I've accumulated over the years, it's worth reminding myself that I was in no great shape when I started off, and in many ways I'm now probably in better shape than I was then. Obviously I dance very differently now and I dance very different kinds of work. I couldn't dance some of the ballet stuff if I tried, (which I don't!). I wouldn't be able to jump as well as I could once, and I don't often try – I couldn't do a lot of classical-type jumping or even Cossack-type jumping, for example. There are things I wouldn't do now.

Jacky: Do you think they are the kinds of things only very young dancers can do?

Fergus: I don't know. It was interesting some years ago, when we performed *Tales from the Citadel*,[14] and I took it upon myself to bring in this classical enchaînement with brisés volés and things that I hadn't done for about 20 years. When I started to do that, I thought God! This is going to be impossible. But once I'd done it a little while, I was actually doing quite respectable petit batterie. In fact, if one kept doing it, there's probably quite a lot of ballet technique one could do. It's partly because I have no particular desire or reason to do anything like that anyway. Though there are things in classical ballet like jumping and landing with that degree of turn-out, which are tough on the body, you know. To land on one leg after a jumping turn can be a very strong wrench on the knee, for example, and I'd be very reluctant to try that sort of thing at all now.

I notice that training for things is very specific. If you want to do ballet, you have to train ballet, really hard. If you want to play cricket, you'll use completely different muscles than you'll use for dancing, or for swimming or for walking. I think if you want to do a thing well, you have to do it a lot. There's basic fitness – making sure that your heart's in good shape, that your big muscle groups are functioning well and are stretched and so on, and that does help a lot – I find I can dance quite vigorously if I've been doing plenty of running and stretching – but there are specific things that will make me very sore, whatever the dance is.

Jacky: Do you think your dance vocabulary has extended? Can you do things now that you couldn't do then?

Fergus: Yes. Lots of things. They're mostly to do with the ability to be fluid in the centre of me. To be much more mobile in the hip area, the lower back area. What ballet did was to give you a terrific central strength, from a hold in the middle. When I work with young students and I see that they haven't got any of that strength, I realize that it's quite important. But at the same time I can now use a range of movement that I wouldn't have touched as a ballet dancer. It's to do with a more released action, specifically around the lower spine and the pelvis. Also, much more grounded movement. So now I'm comfortable with movement that is closer to jazz or African or other forms of dance. I was always a character dancer so I always did a lot of national or folk dances, but they tended to be quite balleticized, and still have that hold and lift up, but I feel I can approach other kinds of more grounded movement now.

Jacky: I think the whole thing of training in depth in other techniques is quite complex for people like you and me who studied for so many years as children – so that to decide as an adult to place yourself back in that position is quite hard.

Fergus: Yes. Perhaps in that way it's not necessary in a sense – your body knows a lot of things.

Jacky: Yes, and one of the things you acquire is the ability to memorize very well, isn't it?

Fergus: That's exactly right. The acquisition of that skill of learning fast is crucial because then it means you gain very quickly in other circumstances. In my life I've sometimes had to teach a lot of roles and dances to people. I got to the point where I could look at someone dancing a role and learn it, just from looking at it. I could teach it to someone else without ever having danced it. I think that's meant that I could absorb different styles quite easily, sometimes without even practically experiencing them. Maybe that's why my choreographic 'style' is so eclectic.

Jacky: So how do you train now? How do you keep fit?

Fergus: Well. If I'm rehearsing, I work out myself in the studio; I normally start out by 5–10 minutes' running, just to warm up; I do a lot of stretches, then a few exercises specially for my stomach, my upper body and the backs of my legs, which I feel need a bit of extra work; then the rest is just to do with rehearsing. If I'm not rehearsing and I just want to keep a level of fitness going, I try to get either to the park and run and swim and stretch, or go into the studio and do a warm-up, some strengthening exercises, then some stretches. I tend to do that more in the winter, when outdoor running is less pleasant, though recently a new heated outdoor swimming pool has opened near me (I dislike indoor pools) and that has meant that I can comfortably swim a decent amount all the year round. I don't do vast amounts: I tend to do 10–15 minutes' run, 20 minutes' exercise and 15 minutes' swim, for example, and not necessarily daily – three or four times a week if I'm not rehearsing. The other thing I do is ride a bicycle a lot, I cycle to work in London and use the bike for most short and medium journeys.

Jacky: So you feel you have to do that much to maintain a level of fitness?

Fergus: Yes. The other thing I do is a certain amount of teaching, sometimes quite a lot, sometimes not so much, but I do a lot of physical work when I teach, joining in with the people I'm teaching. But there are periods when I have a hell of a lot of administrative work, or head work of one sort or another and I find it hard to fit in enough physical exercise. That's always a danger moment for me. Generally I manage to injure myself when I'm not working very fully physically. If I can keep working fully physically, I don't get many injuries.

Jacky: Has it taken to this point to organize that training process, to know what you need?

Fergus: Yes. I suppose it is a process of evolution; my regime has grown up around my life-style and the particular demands of my work. It's not definitive – I often add new stretches or exercises when I meet them and find them useful. The other thing I do in the summer is play cricket. Once a week. Cricket is funny, because sometimes you expend a huge amount of energy, running after the ball all the time or you're lucky enough to bat for a long time, which involves a lot of running up and down very fast, and sometimes you have a day when the ball hardly comes your way, or you're out first ball when you're batting, or you don't get to bowl and you do comparatively little. But at the very least you're about 5 hours standing around and walking about with a certain amount of running around in the open air.

Jacky: A lot of what you've just described sounds completely different from your early experience, which was all to do with the social context, the hierarchical structures, the roles you performed. What you've just described (apart from the cricket) is a much more internal physical process. It's also quite an individualized, solitary process. You've left out the notion of going to class, which was what you would have done in the early days and which is very much a communal activity. It probably takes the maturity of age to be able to work with such a solitary process.

Fergus: That's probably right, though I think it would be wrong to say there weren't some deep internal processes going on, even as a ballet dancer. In a class you are nevertheless on your own, in a way, and I do remember intense internal dialogues with myself as a ballet dancer in a class. So the situation was not purely social. But yes, I probably couldn't have sustained anything like the way I work now. Then again, I've always toured, from a very early age and so I've often had to do my own class out on tour. I think, funnily enough I learnt quite young how to work on my own, because I had to.

Jacky: On the other hand, the communal class can give you energy.

Fergus: And terrific to have a teacher, if it's a good teacher. My problem is that I just dislike most classes so much.

Jacky: All the things you have described, like cricket, running and swimming in the park, sound pleasurable. Do you think pleasure is the key thing?

Fergus: I think I find considered movement deeply pleasurable. I always have, and I continue to – movement that has a purpose, that I think about. That's one of my great pleasures in life.

Jacky: What was your earliest memory of that?

Fergus: What springs to my mind is a wooden playpen that used to be put out on the grass and I remember the pleasure of working out how to get through the little square opening it had, getting my body to manoeuvre itself through so I could get out of the playpen.

Then the sea, swimming, learning to swim. And doing things for a long time. I love doing things for a long time. I suppose it's kind of meditative. When I was about 12 or 13, at White Lodge[15] I decided I wanted to run round the whole of Richmond Park, about 7 or 8 miles. I'd never run anything like that distance before, and I just set off, all on my own on a Sunday and ran the whole way round. There's certainly a real pleasure for me in the emotional journey that accompanies a long physical journey.

Jacky: What are some of the recent performing experiences that have given you most pleasure?

Fergus Early in *Holding Space*, choreographed by Jacky Lansley, at the Clore Studio, Royal Opera House, London, 2004.
Photograph: Hugo Glendinning

Fergus: Well, in general the thing that most excites me is putting together a character – I love the dancing side of things, but it satisfies me most when that's part of creating a person on stage, the gesture, the way of walking, all the detail. I've always felt that way, from the earliest days in ballet right up to, for example, dancing the role of The Employer in your piece *Bird*.[16] I particularly like making people laugh – I think it's the audible feedback, knowing you've done something which an audience is surprised by but also deeply recognizes. Other things can be terrifically pleasurable, the soaring or the spinning or whatever, but they don't actually *need* an audience to be enjoyable. Character and comedy seem to be near the heart of performing, at least for me. Even in fairly abstract pieces, like your *Holding Space* which was very enjoyable in pure dance terms, I found a sort of vestigial character which I think enriched the performance.

The other thing I've been enjoying recently is singing as part of performing. I've always used song as part of the shows I make for Green Candle, but only fairly recently have I allowed myself to sing solo. I'm not a great singer, but I can just about hold a tune and I find the challenge and the extra dimension it gives to performance quite exciting. My latest show for Green Candle, *Falling About*[17], is the story of a woman's life through the metaphor of falling, and I act as narrator, talking and singing as well as dancing.

Jacky: What are you working on at the moment?

Fergus: At the moment I'm planning a large-scale community show to take place in a park next door to the building we're based in in Bethnal Green. We do a lot of work with non-professional older people and also with young people up to the age of about 20. So I want to bring some of these groups together, along with some professional dancers and musicians in an open-air performance piece called *Threads*, that charts the successive waves of immigration to the East End of London – Protestant Huguenots from France in the seventeenth century, East European Jews in the late nineteenth century and Bangladeshi people over the past 40 years. Part of the plan is to work with a landscape architect to leave a permanent outdoor performing area in the park, so that's really exciting.

Jacky: How important do you think dance is to the world?

Fergus: More and more I think it is literally vital. It's the life force. Green Candle is based on the idea that everyone has the right to watch and participate in dance and although we are not really in the business of *persuading* people to dance, we do offer many people who wouldn't ordinarily have the chance an *opportunity* to dance. So I see very young children dance, I see very frail older people dance, I see sick children and disabled adults and every kind of person dance and it is clear to me that it is something essential to all our humanity.

Cornwall, UK, August 2010, developed from an earlier interview in 1998

Notes

1. Schuhplattler: a dance from the Austrian Tyrol which involves rhythmic clapping and slapping of body and legs.
2. Teresa Early: founded and ran Balletmakers Ltd., in London in the early 60s – an organization to provide young choreographers, designers and composers support and a platform to present new work at a time when there were no other avenues for choreographic development in the United Kingdom. Later founded New Peckham Varieties – now Theatre Peckham – offering high quality arts education and training to children and young people residing in and around the London borough of Southwark.
3. Ballet for All: founded by Peter Brinson, it was an educational off-shoot of the Royal Ballet, touring to schools and small theatres with programmes that showed aspects of the history and development of ballet, first as lecture-demonstrations and later as 'ballet-plays' performed by dancers and actors.
4. Peter Brinson (1920–95): dance critic, film-maker, he was for a time Director of the UK branch of the Gulbenkian Foundation and Director of the Royal Academy of Dancing. He was author of the first dance policy ever adopted by a political party in this country (Labour, in 1992).
5. *La Fille Mal Gardée*: three-act ballet, danced by the Royal Ballet in a version choreographed by Frederick Ashton.
6. Gulbenkian Foundation: The Calouste Gulbenkian Foundation is a charitable foundation established in Portugal in 1956 and with branches in London and Paris. Its interests are cultural, educational, social and scientific.
7. Patricia Hutchinson MacKenzie: dance teacher who, as the first principal of the London School of Contemporary Dance was instrumental, along with founder Robin Howard and Artistic Director Robert Cohan, in shaping the school from its establishment in 1969.
8. Sally Potter: film director who worked with Jacky Lansley and later Rose English as performance art group Limited Dance Company in the 1970s.
9. Di Davies: performance artist who worked for some years with Welfare State International and was a founder member of IOU Theatre.
10. X6 Dance Space: dance studio and performance space 1976–81, founded by a collective of Emilyn Claid, Maedée Duprès, Fergus Early, Jacky Lansley and Mary Prestidge. An enlarged version of this collective founded *New Dance* magazine, 1977–88.
11. Mary Fulkerson: US dancer, choreographer and teacher who ran the Dance Course in the Theatre Department of Dartington College in the seventies and eighties and then founded the Center for New Dance Development in Arnhem, Holland. Now based in the United States.
12. Contact Improvisation: a form of dance developed by Steve Paxton and others in the early 1970s that utilizes the physical laws of friction, momentum, gravity and inertia to explore the relationship between dancers.
13. Green Candle Dance Company: founded by Fergus Early in 1987, the company works mainly in community and educational settings in the United Kingdom and has been a pioneer in its work with children, older adults, disabled people and deaf children and young people, including 9 years of the Deaf Dance Summer School, under the direction of Green Candle's then Associate Director, Rachel Elliott.
14. *Tales from the Citadel* (1996): production by Green Candle Dance Company. See Introduction.
15. White Lodge: Junior Royal Ballet School, for pupils aged 11–16.
16. *Bird* (2001): a dance play, derived from the ballet, *The Firebird*, written and choreographed by Jacky Lansley.
17. *Falling About* (2008): choreographed by Fergus Early, music by Martina Schwarz, design by Nina Ayres. Created for older audiences in day care centres, hospitals, village halls etc.

Afterthoughts

Jacky Lansley and Fergus Early

In the course of collecting these interviews, we visited several artists in their studios and it confirmed for us the importance of place and space. There are small dance studios all over the world. Improvisation and adaptability have allowed imaginative dancers, like our contributors, to see the potential in the rural and urban architectural detritus of the twentieth and twenty-first centuries. Will Gaines manages to encapsulate this sense of creative making do better than anyone when he says 'I got a shed, and a lot of wood, and I'm going to lay that down.' These spaces may be barns and farm buildings, garages, offices, houses, factories, converted warehouses, lofts. Sometimes the 'studio' will simply be a designated area under the shade of trees.

Research into new dance languages, vocabularies and processes, rather than slavish commitment to one technique or style, is at the core of the work in these studios, linking them to the tradition of the artist's studio – whether that of a painter, sculptor, film-maker, photographer or choreographer – rather than the institution. While everyone knows that dance requires *rehearsal* studios, it is not commonly understood that the dancer or choreographer needs a studio to research ideas and language – how many times has one been asked 'what do you actually do in your studio?' In fact the tradition of the small independent studio is ancient: in Japan, in every city there are hidden studios where Noh, Kabuki and Nihon Buyo masters rehearse, make dances and plays and receive their students. These studios are not funded – a common theme – and their inherited artefacts, kimonos, musical instruments and masks, are taxed quite heavily. Despite this they are spaces dedicated to the practice of dance where choreographing new work is still very much alive.

Some urban studios have been around for decades, joining up a delicate global network of dance artists, techniques and processes; such a one is Pauline de Groot's studio in Amsterdam, synonymous with the birth of independent dance practice in the Netherlands, where she has been creating work and teaching for over 40 years. Some studios are purpose built in rural contexts – such as Steve Paxton and Lisa Nelson's beautiful studio in the mountains of Vermont, which they built themselves from local timber. Julyen Hamilton's studio, out of which he has been working for 25 years, is a converted pigsty in northern

Yasuo Imai, doyen of Japanese Noh performers, in his studio in Tokyo, Japan, 2010. Photograph: Yoko Nishimura

Spain, and Philippe Priasso's company, Beau Geste, works from an exquisite studio in rural Normandy, France.

Several of the experienced dancers who have contributed to this book emerged from the radicalism and diversity of a 'young' postmodern movement and in their later careers remain among today's most progressive dance artists. However it has not necessarily been easy. Some have struggled to find a clear context for their work as it may defy artistic categorization or collide with a world of professional dance that insists on clinging to old methods and ideologies; all have had their economic challenges. Despite these realities it is important to understand that this vibrant independent sector has not resulted from artists 'dropping out' of some actual or notional mainstream dance world; on the contrary, they have chosen to create and be part of an alternative professional context that has within its practices the resources to be part of much broader cultural fields, encompassing a wide variety of people, disciplines and social issues.

Most importantly this book is for younger generations of practitioners who want and need to see their work and training as part of a real professional context that has depth. With the proliferation of dance and performance degrees there are hundreds of young people emerging from universities who want to enter this world of independent dance practice and who need to see and learn from the work of previous generations of artists who have helped to establish it; they want to be inspired by the broader disciplines and experiences of these artists and by the idea that it might be possible to have a career at least as long as other professions and probably even longer.

Although age is a defining feature of this book, precisely governing whom we chose to interview, the overwhelming impression these interviews give is of vigorous and questing minds and bodies, still 'growing new patterns from a new imagination' as Lisa Nelson says of herself. In the end, paradoxically, it is not the age of these dancers or any struggle they may have to live with the ageing process that is most interesting: it is their ongoing practice as artists. On a personal level it has been deeply pleasurable to have had the opportunity to work with the other artists who have contributed to this book; all have been extraordinarily generous with their time and patient with the long process towards completion. We have lived with this project on and off for several years and it has been a constant source of inspiration and delight. For all of us dance is a way of life – an attitude distilled by the great octogenarian Noh performer Yasuo Imai who suggested to us 'If you're an artist, there is so much to do – you have to live a long time to do it.'

Biographies

Philippe Priasso

Philippe was born in Saint-Étienne, France, in 1957. He was destined for a scientific career but abandoned studies in biology to devote himself to contemporary dance. In 1978, after a workshop run by the US choreographer Alwin Nikolais in Avignon, he joined the Centre National de Danse Contemporaine (CNDC) in Anger, under Nikolais' direction, first as a student, then as a dancer in the company directed by Nikolais.

In 1981, he co-founded the company Beau Geste with four other dancers from the CNDC and has remained with the company ever since, as choreographer, dancer and teacher. As a teacher, he has developed a personal style based on the Nikolais technique. His choreography includes collective work with other members of Beau Geste, solo pieces, choreography for theatre, musicals and opera. Since 2005, he has been touring all over the world with *Transports Exceptionnels*, a duet for a dancer and a mechanical digger, choreographed by Dominique Boivin, Artistic Director of Beau Geste.

For Philippe, dance is a performing art which must establish a unique link with the audience. His concern is to find the form which will make it easiest to read or perceive the idea behind the choreography – he does not adhere to a specific style, but as a choreographer he aims to involve the physical and movement personalities of the dancers who are creating the work, while still remaining uncompromising in his role of making the movement clear and therefore readable and accessible.

Lisa Nelson

Lisa Nelson is a choreographer, improvisational performer, videographer and collaborative artist who has been exploring the role of the senses in the performance of movement since the early 1970s. Collaboration and improvisation, with methods rooted in dialogue and survival, have been her constant companions.

She trained in traditional modern dance and ballet as a child at the Juilliard School in New York City, and received a degree in Dance from Bennington College in 1971. In pursuit of a flexible movement language, she studied world music, western music (piano and guitar), mime, T'ai Chi, experimental theatre (Open Theater), experiential anatomy with Bonnie Bainbridge Cohen at the School for Body-Mind Centering and the perceptual research of J. J. Gibson.

Throughout the 1970s she investigated diverse approaches to dance improvisation, including solo; collaboration with musicians; performance with Daniel Nagrin's Workgroup in New York City – exploring dramatic qualities of movement interaction; and performance with various contact improvisation groups in the United States and in Europe.

Nelson's work in performance and teaching questions the methods of transmission of movement through the senses to the conscious and subconscious experience within the dancer, between dancers, from dancer to viewer, within the viewer. She asks, 'When you watch me dance, are you improvising?' This question led her to create a 2-year course of study in video for dancers at Bennington College.

Stemming from this investigation with video and dance, she developed an approach to spontaneous composition and dance performance she calls Tuning Scores. Throughout the1990s she developed these scores for interdisciplinary performance with the group Image Lab, including Scott Smith, Karen Nelson and K. J. Holmes, offering site-specific 'Observatories' in countries across Europe, the Americas, China, Australia, Israel. Nelson continues to gather international artists to participate in Observatories and visits ongoing Tuning practice groups here and there.

Her long-term collaborations with other performing artists include dancers Steve Paxton (*PA RT; Night Stand*), Daniel Lepkoff (*Salt-talks; Ball Room*) Scott Smith (*GO*) and video artist/choreographer Cathy Weis (*An Abondanza in the Air*).

Since 1977, she has co-edited and contributed writing to *Contact Quarterly*, international dance and improvisation journal (www.contactquarterly.com), and directs Videoda, a production, archival and distribution project for videotapes of improvised dance. Her writings have been published in numerous international dance publications including *Dance Theatre Journal, BalletTanz, Nouvelles de Danse* and *Writings on Dance*. In 2001, she was contributing editor to *Vu du Corps: Lisa Nelson, Mouvement et Perception, Nouvelles de Danse* #48–49 Brussels (in French).

She lives on a farm in Vermont in the United States.

La Tati

La Tati was born in Madrid and learned to dance by stealthily observing La Quica's classes. She made her debut at the age of 12 in the tablao Zambra in Madrid where she danced for three seasons with important flamenco figures such as Pericon de Cadiz, Juan Varea, Rafael Romero, Perico el del Lunar and Rosa Durán. Between 1960 and 1965 she worked with the company at Torres Bermejas in Madrid, sharing the stage with, among others, Camarón de la Isla, Niño Ricardo, Fernanda and Bernarda Utrera and La Paquera de Jerez.

From 1966 to 1975 she toured to many parts of the world with the Lusillo Dance Theatre and others. From 1976 to 1984 she performed at the Sevillian tablao 'La Trocha' as well as at the great Andalusian festivals such as La Parpuja, El Poaje de Utrera and the Fiesta de la Buleria of Jerez. She was invited to teach at the National Ballet of Spain under the direction of Antonio.

From 1985 to 1987 she took part in two productions of the Cumbre Flamenca Festival, toured with the Cumbre Flamenca Festival company and formed her own company. In 1988 and 1989 she had a great success at the Cirque d'Hiver in Paris together with Camarón de la Isla. She premiered her work *Apologia Flamenco* at the Theatre Sodra in Stockholm, which she later presented at the Mogador in Paris and at the Teatro Nuevo Apolo in Madrid. In the 1990s she continued to tour and formed her own production company. In 1996 she worked as choreographer and director of the fifteenth Guitar Festival of Israel. In 1997 she premiered her show *Madrí-Jeré* in Madrid and in 1998 she took part in Campanas Flamencas as soloist and choreographic co-ordinator.

In 2000 she formed a new company called Flamenco Theatre of La Tati to debut her production of *La Casa de Bernada Alba* from the play by Federico Garcia Lorca. Her current show (2010) is called *Relumbre, Rojo Robre Morado* a geographic tour of the cantes, from different parts of Spain. Her next project will be *Madre Coraje* – a flamenco version of Brecht's *Mother Courage*.

Julyen Hamilton

Julyen is a dancer, choreographer, poet and teacher. He has been making dances for over 35 years, performing dance work throughout the world. Born and brought up in England, he trained in London in the 1970s, a time of radical theatre experimentation. After early experiences in theatre he started dancing at the age of 19 in Cambridge with Liebe Klug, subsequently working with Rosemary Butcher and Richard Alston. He has been an exponent of innovative performance since that time.

His work is mostly improvised: he composes dance pieces instantly as well as the texts which often accompany them. When choreographing with his company *Allen's Line* he directs dancers and lighting designers to make and perform work through this same immediacy.

Since the 1980s he has performed in collaboration with many live musicians from all over Europe, including Michael Moore, Fred Frith, Malcolm Goldstein, Daniel Humair, Alfred Spirli, Xavier Garcia, Christian Reiner, Wilbert de Joode, Marjolaine Charbin, Vladimir Volkov, Tristan Honsinger, Sebi Tramontana, Axel Dörninger. It is with some of these musicians that he gives readings of his poetry.

He is well respected for his teaching which reflects his research and development into efficient ways in which improvisational creativity can evolve and technique skills might be imparted. He is regularly invited to teach in major training centres throughout the world, his pedagogy centring on the elements of space, time, voice and dramaturgy.

He is currently presenting the solos *How It Is Made* and *The Immaterial World*, performing duos with bass players Barre Phillips and Jean-Claude Jones, working with Ritsche Koch (live painting, dance and music) in Berlin and with his own company in Brussels. His label *BLUE DOG DVDs* produces videos of his performances on DVD. A CD of his music and poetry is planned for release in 2011 on the Sybil Sings label in Holland.

Yoshito Ohno

Yoshito Ohno was born in 1938 in Tokyo and began to dance from a young age as a student of his father Kazuo Ohno. His first stage appearance was in 1959 when he appeared in his father's stage adaptation of Ernest Hemingway's *The Old Man and the Sea*. In the same year he danced the role of a young boy *Kinjiki* in Tatsumi Hijikata's controversial adaptation of Yukio Mishima's *Forbidden Colours*, which is taken as the first creation of Butoh in its history. During the 1960s he was a prominent participant in Hijikata's experiments working with his group Ankoku Butoh-ha. He retired from public performance in 1969 and was not to reappear in performance until he co-performed with his father in *The Dead Sea* in 1985. Following the death of Hijikata in 1986 Yoshito took charge of directing his father's creations, notably *Water Lilies* (1987), and *Flower-Birds-Wind-Moon* (1990). In the mid-1990s he embarked on a solo career; his recitals include The *Last Picture of Dorian Gray* inspired by Oscar Wilde's novel.

In parallel with his performing career, Yoshito Ohno is an established teacher and regularly gives master classes throughout the world. He is based at the Kazuo Ohno Studio in Yokohama, Japan, where he teaches and makes work. He is the joint author with Kazuo of several books including *Kazuo Ohno's World: from without and within*. Yoshito is currently performing and touring his most recent solo recital, which explores holocaust.

Steve Paxton

Steve Paxton has researched the fiction of cultured dance and the 'truth' of improvisation for 40 years. He began his career studying modern dance techniques, ballet, Aikido, T'ai Chi Chuan, and Vipassana meditation. He performed with the Merce Cunningham Dance Company from 1961–65 and was one of an informal group of dancers who formed the Judson Dance Theater, often considered the founders of postmodern dance. He was also one of the originators of Grand Union, the influential dance improvisation group of the 1970s, in New York. In 1972 he named and began to develop the dance form known as Contact Improvisation, a form of dance that utilizes the physical laws of friction, momentum, gravity and inertia to explore the relationship between dancers. With Anne Kilcoyne he founded Touchdown Dance in the United Kingdom for the visually disabled. He is a contributing editor to *Contact Quarterly* dance journal. He lectures, performs, choreographs and teaches primarily in the United States and Europe.

In 2008, he and Lisa Nelson performed *Night Stand* in Spain, and he published a DVD with ContreDanse in Brussels. In 2009 he re-choreographed *Ave Nue* (1985) in Amsterdam, and toured Japan, including *Night Stand* in Tokyo. With ContreDanse of Brussels, he, Florence Corin and Baptiste Andrien have developed the *Phantom Exhibition*, a multi-image room of meditations on *Material for the Spine*, recently recognized by the Japan Media Arts Festival.

He lives on a farm in Vermont, United States, and he has received grants from Change, Inc., the Foundation for Performance Arts, John D.Rockefeller Fund, Contemporary Performance Arts Foundation and a Guggenheim Fellowship. He has been awarded two New York Bessie Awards.

Jacky Lansley

Jacky Lansley's career as a choreographer and dancer has spanned four decades. She forged her unique style from a training in both classical work with the Royal Ballet Company and in the radical worlds of Performance Art and New Dance with diverse collaborators including Sally Potter, with whom she created Limited Dance Company in the 1970s, Rose English, Richard Alston (as a member of Strider), Barry Flanagan, David Medalla, Lynn MacRitchie, Anna Furse, Vincent Meehan, Tim Rubidge, Di Davies, Sylvia Hallett, Mary Fulkerson and with numerous groups and companies including: Helen Jives, The Acme Gallery, Welfare State, The London Musicians' Collective, The Drill Hall, Dance Organisation, Extemporary Dance Theatre, Spiral, English New Dance Theatre, John Bull Puncture Repair Kit, Fluxus, The Women's Playhouse Trust, The Manchester Royal Exchange, The Almeida (with Yuri Lyubimov), The Royal Court Theatre and The Bristol Old Vic Theatre (as a co-director with Lily Susan Todd). She was a founder (with Early, Emilyn Claid, Maedée Duprès, Mary Prestidge) of the UK's radical independent dance studios, X6 Dance Space and Chisenhale Dance Space and in 2002 she founded the Dance Research Studio in London where she is based.

Her choreographic practice combines visual and theatrical disciplines and is concerned with space and the site specific; she has made works in many different kinds of indoor and outdoor environments and one of her most recent projects *View from the Shore* was inspired by the Cornish coastal landscape with which she has had a long-term special relationship. In 2008 she created *Standing Stones* which premiered at York Minster and toured to fourteen UK cathedrals. Her work in film includes choreography and performance in Sally Potter's *The Gold Diggers*, *The London Story*, *Orlando* and *The Man Who Cried*. She has written and directed several short films, including *Through the Fire*, *The Life Class*, *Swaying* and *Who Became Those* (with Fergus Early).

Throughout her working life she has been developing processes and training methods for interdisciplinary performance practice and in 2009 she launched a professional development programme: *The Speaking Dancer: Interdisciplinary Performance Training* (SDIPT) for dancers and actors. She guest lectures widely in dance and performance and is an associate lecturer at the University of Plymouth in the United Kingdom. She was a founder and editor of the seminal *New Dance* magazine, and has written extensively on dance and performance including articles for *Performance Research*, *The Open Page*, *Dance Theatre Journal* and the British Film Institute. In 2010 she received awards from the Daiwa and Sasakawa Foundations to support a research trip to Japan and is currently developing a new ensemble work inspired by Japanese Noh theatre.

Will Gaines

Will Gaines is the last in a long line of Jazz Hoofers (tap dancers). He was born in Baltimore in 1928. He grew up in Detroit where he learned his craft with such greats as Lucky Thompson, Kenny Burrel, Tommy Flanagan and Sonny Stitt.

At the age of 20 he saw the Duke Ellington and Count Basie Orchestras, Dizzy Gillespie and Billie Holiday. In New York in 1957 he joined Cab Calloway's Cotton Club Show, Martha

Raye's Night Club in Miami, danced in Las Vegas and Washington DC where he performed in front of President Eisenhower and finally in Central Park, Manhattan, NY.

He went on the road again in 1958, opening the show at the 500 Club in Atlantic City, working with, among others, Martha Raye, Eartha Kitt, Lena Horne, Nat King Cole and Sammy Davis Junior.

He was one of a small group of tap dancers who took tap from being an exhibition form – the 'buck and wing' of vaudeville – to an expressive form – rhythm tap – where the dancer became an integral part of the music. Will has always considered himself to be a musician first and a dancer second.

He arrived in London in 1963, appearing at the Pigalle, Ronnie Scott's and, in 1964, the Palladium with Norman Vaughan, Tommy Cooper and the Jack Parnell Orchestra.

Going back to his jazz roots, he worked with such well-known names as Alex Walsh, Tony Lee, George Chisholm, Tony Oxley, Stan Tracey, Humphrey Lyttelton and John Stevens. He is equally at home dancing with mainstream bands as he is with an avant-garde improviser like the late guitarist Derek Bailey, with whom he made a video. He has appeared at the Royal Festival Hall and the Queen Elizabeth Hall as well as festivals throughout the United Kingdom, including Glasgow, Edinburgh, Bracknell and Birmingham. Will's TV appearances range from *Playschool* to *Top of the Pops* and he is the only American Jazz Hoofer to perform at the Royal Opera House. Well into his 80s, he lives and continues to perform regularly in the United Kingdom.

Pauline de Groot

Pauline de Groot's early training and dance experience in the United States (1957–65) with Martha Graham, José Limón, Merce Cunningham, Erick Hawkins and André Bernard established her kinship with the Judson Church generation and her roots in the American avant-garde.

On her return to the Netherlands in 1965, she introduced new ideas about movement and aesthetics, and in 1968 founded a school in her studio that later formed the foundation of the School for New Dance Development of the Amsterdam School of Higher Education in the Arts. As one of the main teachers at the SNDD for 20 years, Pauline de Groot was an influence on several generations of dancers and makers in the field today.

Pauline has integrated in her work principles of movement disciplines, such as T'ai Chi, Chi Kung, Todd Alignment, Alexander Technique, Release Technique and Contact Improvisation. The performance of improvisation is essential in her work: 'improvisation is a craft needing scrutiny and devotion…' Her work moves from the dance of rolling and flying to the dance of stillness and awareness.

Of great influence to her life and work have been the teachings of the Buddha, first through Tibetan masters Trungpa Rinpoche and Sogyal Rinpoche and more recently through Zen master Thich Nat Hahn. In the wide field of movement, dance and meditation, the exchange and performances with colleagues, such as Australian choreographer Russell Dumas, Indonesian movement and meditation master Suprapto Suryodarmo, the study of Zhan Zhuang Chi Kung with Peter den Dekker and his master Lam Kam Chuen, the practice of Sacred Clowning with Didier Danthois and various projects with students, dancers, actors, musicians, clowns and storytellers, continue to challenge and inform her work.

Jane Dudley

Dudley had her roots in the left theatre movement of early 1930s United States that spilled over to dance. A founder, in 1932, of the New Dance Group, which performed in union halls and factories, her aim was to make dance accessible to a non-dance audience and to offer material with a political orientation.

In 1935 she performed in Martha Graham's *Panorama* after which she continued to perform with the Martha Graham Company for 11 years. She also taught in the Martha Graham School in New York from 1938–58. Her rich and varied career as a dancer, choreographer and teacher took her all over the world, making her one of the most recognized and respected contributors to the development of contemporary dance. Her finest choreographic work, much of it engaged with social and political issues, was for the Dudley-Maslow-Bales Trio she formed with Sophie Maslow and William Bales. From 1950 to 1956 she was Director of the New Dance Group Studio and she was Artistic Director of Batsheva Dance Company in Israel from 1968 to 1969. In 1970 she came to the United Kingdom to take up the post of Director of Graham Studies at the newly formed London Contemporary Dance School, retiring in 1990 to resume her career as a performer and choreographer.

Her early choreography included *Harmonica Breakdown, New World A' Comin', Short Story* and *Time is Money*. In later years in the United Kingdom she created work for Extemporary Dance Theatre, Spiral Dance and Phoenix Dance Company. In 1993 she performed *Dances with Music* for Victoria Marks at the International Dance Umbrella Festival and in 1994 she restaged *Harmonica Breakdown* for London Contemporary Dance Theatre. In 1996 she performed in Green Candle Dance Company's production *Tales from the Citadel* on tour and at the Dance Umbrella Festival, and in 1999 she was the subject and choreographer of a film directed by Gillian Lacey – *Dancing Inside*. Jane was awarded an Honorary Doctor of Music Degree from Kent University. She died in September 2001 at the age of 89.

Bisakha Sarker

Bisakha Sarker is a performer, animateur, choreographer and educationalist. She trained in creative and classical Indian dance at the Uday Shankar Culture Centre, Calcutta, run by Smt Amala Shankar. She had further training in choreography from the pioneer of Nava Nritya, Manjusri Chaki-Sircar.

Working in a wide range of situations, her innovative collaborative work – often with disabled people and older people – has challenged traditional cultural boundaries. Bisakha was the first South Asian dance animateur for Merseyside and for more than 25 years has been at the forefront of the development of dance in new contexts in the North West of England and elsewhere.

In her own choreography, she has developed a range of work based on texts written in English. Many of her dances are inspired by Tagore's poems translated by William Radice. As she approached 50, she invited a young choreographer, Shobana Gulati, to choreograph a piece, *Nagar Sangeet*, which enabled her to negotiate the demands of being an older dancer and to find hidden strengths within her own body. This contributed to a new understanding of her emotional and physical involvement with dance as an older performer.

Bisakha is Artistic Director of Chaturangan, a development initiative for South Asian dance in the North West of England which, with support from Merseyside Dance Initiative and the Foundation for Community Dance, has organized two national conferences on Dance and Older People.

She is co-author with François Matarasso of a book – *Making Space* – on South Asian dance and disability and has received a number of awards, including a New Horizon award from the Calouste Gulbenkian Foundation, a Lisa Ullman Travelling Scholarship and a Windsor Scholarship from Arts Council, England.

Since 1984 Bisakha has been actively involved in exploring ways of enriching the sector of dance and ageing. As an independent artist, she has consistently collaborated with other artists and organizations, initiating debate and discussion on this important area of work.

Fergus Early

A leading figure in British New Dance and the Community Dance movement, he began his career with the Royal Ballet in the 1960s. An original member and resident choreographer of the Royal Ballet's Ballet for All company, he left in the early 1970s to study and teach at the London Contemporary Dance School. In 1976, Fergus joined forces with Jacky Lansley, Mary Prestidge, Emilyn Claid and Maedée Duprès to establish X6 Dance Space, the United Kingdom's first independent experimental dance studio and performing space. He was also a founder member of *New Dance* magazine which from 1977–88 was a radical voice for dance in the United Kingdom. In 1981, he was a founder member of Chisenhale Dance Space. Fergus has choreographed works for many companies including Extemporary Dance Theatre, The Kosh, Norwegian National Ballet and the Royal Exchange Theatre, Manchester (where he was an Associate Director), as well as devising and performing several solo shows. In 1981 he collaborated with Jacky Lansley to create the much acclaimed *I, Giselle,* a feminist re-interpretation of the ballet classic. He has also taught and lectured extensively in the United Kingdom and abroad.

In 1987 Fergus founded Green Candle Dance Company, based on the belief that everyone has the right to watch and participate in dance. Green Candle works from its base in East London, creating productions, education projects and training programmes particularly aimed at children and young people and at people aged over 60. As Artistic Director, he has written and choreographed 25 full-length productions for the company in a unique style which usually involves narrative, text and song, as well as dance. He is the recipient of several awards, including two Digital Dance Awards, a Greater London Arts Dance Award and the Time Out/Dance Umbrella Award for Outstanding Artistic Achievement. In 2009 he received an OBE for services to dance and he is a Winston Churchill Fellow for 2010. In 2011 he was made an Honorary Doctor of Arts by De Montfort University, Leicester, United Kingdom.

As well as his work as a founding editor and regular contributor to *New Dance* magazine, Fergus is the co-author of a book *Growing Bolder – a Start-up Guide for Creating Dance with Older People*, and has written articles for many publications, including *Animated* and *Cairon, Revistas de la Danza.*

Index

500 Club, 194

Abeles, Nadya Romanoff, 37
Academy of Indian Dance, 166, 171n.31
Acme Gallery, 193
Actor's Studio, 140n.24
Adam, Adolphe, 114n.25
Adams, Jo Jo, 121
Admiring La Argentina, 81, 84n.1, 85n.12
Ailey, Alvin, 176
Akademi *see* Academy of Indian Dance
Alexander Technique, 147, 155n.18, 194
Allen, Dave, 123, 128n.24
Allen's Line, 191
Almeida Theatre, 109, 193
Almora School, 162
Alston, Richard, 64, 70n.2, 71n14, n.9, 105,
    113n1, n.2, n.3, 191, 193
Amaya, Carmen, 55, 58n.2
American Ballet, 140n.14
American Dance Festival, 91, 102n.6
American Document, 133
American Provincials, 133, 137
An Abondanza in the Air, 190
Anamule Dance, 115n.32
Andrien, Baptiste, 192
Animated, 196
Ankoku Butoh, 77, 79, 81, 85n.12, n.14, 192
Ankoku Buyo (Dance of Utter Darkness), 76,
    84.n.3
Antonio, 190
Apologia Flamenca, 191
Appalachian Spring, 133
Art of Movement Studio, 171n.16

Ascendance Rep, 115n.33
Ashbery, John, 102n.5
Ashley, Robert, 44, 50n.13
Ashton, Frederick, 184n.5
Astaire, Fred, 121, 127n.3
Australian Dance Theatre, 156n.31
Ave Nue, 192
Ayres, Nina, 184n.17

Bach, Johann Sebastian, 95, 112, 115n.34
Bailey, Derek, 125, 128n.32, 194
Balanchine, George, 134, 140n.14, n.16
Bales, William, 139n.8, 195
Ball Room, 190
Ballet for All, 176, 184n.3, 196
Ballet Caravan, 134, 140n.15
Ballet Review, 137, 140n.25
Balletmakers Ltd, 184n.2
Ballets Russes, 113n.5, n.6, 114n.22, 140n.16,
    170n.5
Banner, Christopher, 70n.2, 113n.2
Barrault, Jean-Louis, 79, 84n.10
Basie, Count, 121, 127n.5
Bassey, Shirley, 123
Batsheva Dance Company, 195
Bean, Anne, 115n.35
Beau Geste Company, *18*, 20, 21, 22, *23*, 24,
    25-6, *29*, 33n.4, 187, 189
Beck, Julian, 102n.5
Behn, Aphra, 108, 114n.16
Ben Yakov, Jenn, 151
Bennington College, 38, 49n.3, 189, 190
Bennington School of Dance, 139n.5
Bennington Summer School, 132, 139n.5